The Chicago Phoenix

The Chicago Phoenix

JIMMY KEENE'S UNTOLD STORY

JAMES KEENE

SGM

To protect the privacy of individuals when required the names and identifying details have been changed.

Some of our authors do participate in speaking arrangements. If interested, please visit the website below.
www.sillygoatmedia.com

Library of Congress Cataloging-in-Publication Data

Keene, James, 1963–
The Chicago Phoenix: Jimmy Keene's Untold Story / James Keene
—1st ed.
ISBN: 978-1-961181-01-4

First Edition: April 2023

Dedicated in loving memory to
James "Big Jim" Keene, Lynn Keene, and Kevin Corrigan

CONTENTS

AN OUTLAW JAMES BOND

The guard showed up outside my cell early Monday morning in the middle of my exercise routine.

"Keene, you have a visitor. Let's go!"

"Who is it? It's not visiting hours."

"Do I look like your secretary? Move it."

I walked over to the door and turned around to be cuffed. As we headed down the corridor, we passed the hallway toward the visitor's center, and I felt my adrenaline spike. In here you never knew who was on whose list. The guards could be taking you to "talk" with another prisoner, which was never a good thing. As we went around the corner, I saw two guards outside of a small conference room. *Great, here we go again.* Had to be the Feds.

I sat down in the room where I was joined by my lawyer, Steinbeck, and several law officials. We waited for what seemed an eternity, and the reality that something was coming began to settle in my gut.

I asked myself, *Now what do these fuckers want? How many times do I have to tell them I'm not a snitch? I'll never give them names.*

Finally, in walked the prosecutor, Lawrence Beaumont, with his thousand-dollar briefcase, shiny suit, and military buzz cut. There was a guy with him, an FBI agent named Ken Temples, only I didn't know that yet. I'd seen eyes like Ken's over a fan of poker cards, flat and hard, always searching for the advantage.

Beaumont was an intimidating man as well. His piercing blue eyes seemed to look down into your soul and know if you were lying even before you decided what was coming out of your mouth.

Beaumont sat across from me and slid an accordion-folder police file across the table—a three-dimensional resume of crimes and misdemeanors. I raised both my cuffed hands to open it, and when I did, my heart stopped.

I don't know what I expected—maybe some grainy, long-distance photos of drug dealers, or some other "evidence" the Feds thought they had against me. Instead, I was looking at a photo of a dead girl. Naked. In a cornfield. There were ugly purple bruises up and down her legs and across her ribcage. She had a necklace of smaller bruises around her throat. I swallowed. *What are they trying to do, pin this on me, too?*

But I could tell by the look on Beaumont's face there was something more to it. So, I continued going through the file, turning page after page like a high-school yearbook of corpses, some lying face down in ditches, others tossed like a rag doll in a weedy field. The reports were from all over: Indiana, Illinois, Michigan, Wisconsin, Utah.

When I got to the last page, there was a mugshot of some guy named Larry Dewayne Hall. *Wait. Who the hell is Larry Dewayne Hall?*

"You think I know this guy?" I asked Beaumont. "You think I'd ever get mixed up in something like this?"

The grim line of Beaumont's mouth softened a bit. "I know you didn't have anything to do with it, Keene. That's not why you're here."

I closed the file and leaned back, the cuffs clinking as I moved. "Yeah? Then do me a favor and tell me why I'm here."

Beaumont leaned forward and folded his arms on the table between us. "Listen, Keene, I have an offer that will change your life. If you're successful, you'll walk out a free man." He took out another file with the name "Keene" on it. "Let's face it. You're an outlaw James Bond."

I laughed wryly. "That sounds like a compliment."

"I've looked into you, Keene. You have charisma from the street level to the boardroom unlike anyone I've ever seen in my career, you have black-belt martial arts experience, and you've been taught police tactical training and countersurveillance. You gave us the slip for twenty years. You're smart. Superior intelligence. If the circumstances were different, this guy would be trying to recruit you into the FBI." Beaumont's eyes briefly flicked toward Temples.

"What does that have to do with anything?" I said, still trying to figure out what the hell was going on.

"Keene, I want you to transfer to a maximum-security prison in Springfield, Missouri, that houses many of the country's worst criminally insane inmates. That guy is there for killing one of these girls. I know he's killed these other women, but we can't prove it." Beaumont looked at me hard and steady with concern etched deeply into his face.

Was this a joke? I thought Beaumont knew how things worked in lockup. Inmates didn't go around confessing things. Everyone knew prison walls had ears. He might as well have asked me to call the governor about getting myself a pardon.

Beaumont surveyed my silence and continued. "If Hall gets a chance to file an appeal, he may win it due to certain clerical errors. We can't risk that under any circumstances."

"Okay, but I still don't understand. Don't you have trained officers or FBI agents that can do that? Why me?"

Beaumont opened the file of crime-scene photos again, the sly bastard, and pushed it toward me so I'd have to see all those poor dead girls. "I have one shot at this," he said. His voice was gruff and determined. "I can't risk sending in an agent. If he's made, that's it. Hall will walk free on his appeal and continue killing. The families of these girls will never get the closure they need. Hall is cagey, and trust me—he would spot any of these guys as an agent."

"Yeah, but—"

"Listen to me," Beaumont said. "You wouldn't've made it as long as you did if you weren't smart. You can handle yourself in prison. Just get him talking, Keene. That's all. Earn his trust, and he'll tell you everything we need to know."

The room went quiet like they were all waiting for my answer. I looked over at Temples and then back to Beaumont. Agreeing to infiltrate a maximum-security prison as an operative was about the stupidest thing a man could do, but I had ten-to-life weighing on me. I wouldn't give Beaumont the satisfaction of watching me look at those photos, but I knew they were there—a whole file full of lives snuffed out before they'd started.

I didn't know it yet, but I soon found out that what Beaumont was suggesting had never been attempted before—a civilian had never been sent to a maximum-security prison to get a serial killer to confess to anything. And it hasn't been attempted since—it's been legally banned. He'd taken the idea of assigning me to this mission to the United States Department of Justice five times, and they'd turned it down over concerns about my safety. He'd approached them about it a sixth time, and somehow, he'd managed to convince them.

But that's the part of my story everyone knows, and I want to tell the rest. I want to tell how the hell I got into that situation in the first place—the crippling poverty and crime I grew up with that led me to sell marijuana at thirteen years old, my never-ending thirst for that big score that would buy me comfort and luxury for the rest of my life, and the dangerous twenty years I endured in the marijuana business surviving shootouts, dealing with cartels, and evading law enforcement. But that was just the start of a white-knuckle ordeal most people couldn't begin to imagine. It was a hell of a ride!

CHAPTER 1

NOT QUITE THE CLEAVERS

Looking from the outside in, we were the perfect family with a nice house and a couple of Cadillacs in the driveway. We seemed to "keep up with the Joneses," but for us to do that on my dad's civil-servant salary we had to work—and work hard. Ends never seemed to meet without a struggle.

My dad, Big Jim, always wanted a family—a beautiful wife and a couple of kids to throw around a ball with. A house on a hill with a picket fence, a nice car, and even a dog or two would complete the picture. It was an ideal dream! Back then, everybody knew about *Leave it to Beaver*. The Cleaver household was perfect, and everyone wanted that picture of harmony and success for themselves. Too bad it was also make-believe.

Dad met my mom, Lynn, when she was eighteen. She was everything a man would want in a woman: knock-out gorgeous, smart, and a hard worker. They fell in love and were married within a year, and I came soon after. With Dad working on the police force, there wasn't much money coming in to support us, so Mom went back to waiting tables soon after I was born.

She didn't work at some little diner down the road. No, she worked in big, fancy restaurants attached to lounges and hotels. The nightlife in the Chicago area was really something else, and being a beautiful woman was an advantage for a waitress—people would tip well. But it wasn't easy for my parents.

To say I was a handful is an understatement. Nothing slowed me down. I was walking at five-and-a-half months and able to fully run at seven. My mother would take me to work with her and put me in a highchair while she worked to save money on babysitting. Twenty months after I was born, along came my little brother, Timmy. That made things a little more difficult to juggle. Dad was working both at the police department and the fire department. Every third day, he would leave directly after his shift at the police department and go do a twenty-four-hour shift at the fire department.

Our house was on Elm Street, and it felt safe even though it was in the heart of Kankakee. The neighborhood was home to many civil servants like Dad. Even though my parents worked a lot, they spent time with us separately when they could.

Dad never missed any of my sporting events or practices. He was passionate about us boys learning every contact sport there was. We played football and hockey, and we wrestled and practiced in-depth martial arts until we were highly accomplished. We also ran track and played basketball to round it off. I excelled at any sport I decided to put the time into. Along with all of my other sports accomplishments, I eventually lettered in track and competed at State track in three different events every year I ran. I also lettered in football and wrestling. Having two boys in so many sports was not a small expense even back then, but Dad felt it was important. He was right. I used those skills for the rest of my life in one way or another.

My mother had dreams for me too. She wanted me to be a professional saxophone player, so she made sure I practiced every day. She bought me my first saxophone with her hard-earned tips for 365 dollars. In that era, that was a lot—especially for us. That's how much she wanted me to play and become successful. And boy, would I. Before she'd leave for the restaurant at night, she'd come in and say, "Now, let me hear you play something before you do your homework." She didn't care about my other homework. She just cared about the saxophone. I played both the sax and cello for about fourteen years. It broke my mom's heart when I decided to stop and focus on sports.

My mom went to the hair salon every Monday to get her hair teased up real high. She'd load me and my brother into her Cadillac, and we'd go to her friend Josie's hair salon. It took three to five hours to get her hair done, and we'd stay the whole time. The stylists would get us something to eat, and then we'd play with our little toy soldiers. Everywhere we went, my mom was like a movie star. She was so pretty, people gravitated toward her.

Mom was very diligent with her appearance. Her hair and makeup were usually flawless, and she shared those habits with her children. We learned the importance of bathing daily, trimming our nails, and making sure our teeth and hair were always brushed. She taught us to select our clothes and match them. We always looked well cared for at all times, but people didn't realize we did this for ourselves, as young as we were.

One thing Mom taught me that really came in handy was how to sew. I could sew and crochet like the ladies in the neighborhood that had been doing it for twenty years! If someone in the family needed a button put back on a shirt, I did it. If someone had a hole in a sock, I mended it.

I'm not sure how my parents managed to keep their marriage strong as long as they did. They were on alternate shifts almost the whole time they were together, which was not the easiest way to keep the fires burning. Mom was young when she married. She loved us, but I think she felt she missed out on being a young woman. She usually worked swing shift until 3 a.m., and then she stayed around the restaurant to have a drink and relax after work. Dad had to be at work at 6 a.m., and as a policeman or fireman, he couldn't be late. He had to be on time and ready for duty.

Many times, Mom would not come home until Dad loaded us into the car, drove to where she was working, and told her he had to go to work and to please come home and watch the kids. Sometimes, Dad would take us to the police station, and we would sit there on a bench until we got a call that Mom was finally home. Back then, we only had landlines—no pagers, no cell phones. If you couldn't find someone, you either had to wait until they showed up or drive around looking for them.

I think Mom was a victim of her beauty as well as of the unforeseen consequences of her chosen circumstances. She worked hard and barely made ends meet at home. Her after-hours socializing was really the only way she could unwind. It was only too easy for her to use alcohol and cigarettes as a social crutch and a fleeting escape from the responsibilities she carried, and it turned into more of a problem later in her life.

My sister, Terri, was born when I was five and a half. Then, things were even more complicated. Paying for daycare and keeping food on the table and a roof over our heads was a never-ending battle. Both of our parents worked so hard to support us and give us the life they wanted that we were left to our own defenses a lot of the time.

Even after a long shift on her feet, Mom would come home in the summer and take us to the fancy hotel pool where she worked. It was really nice to spend that time with her at the pool and enjoy the summer weather. We would watch the rich people in their swimming suits and all their jewelry sitting around talking, laughing, and drinking cocktails. I wondered what it would be like to have that kind of money. It seemed like they had it all.

After my sister was born, we moved into a home on Skyline Road out in the country. But even though it was surrounded by open space and nature and had a sense of safety, we were only three miles from downtown Kankakee. It even had an amazing orchard with apple, pear, cherry, and peach trees. There was a vineyard and a barn with horses and rabbits. We had dogs and cats. Each of us got our own dog. I picked mine on my birthday at the state police pound.

"Which one you want, son?" I remember Dad asking.

"That one there. He's got really big paws."

He was the biggest puppy of the litter, a black Labrador retriever. When we got home, I asked Dad what we should call him.

Dad said, "How 'bout the Royal Dutchman?" My dad had a unique personality. There was always something different about him.

"*What?* The Royal Dutchman? Who names their dog the Royal Dutchman!" I laughed.

We kept the name but shortened it to "Royal." Because we were in the country, Royal was able to run free. My mom would bring home half-eaten steaks and leftovers from the restaurant for him, and he got big— real big! Royal was 128 pounds, and he was tall like a Doberman and thick like a rottweiler. Royal was a badass dog, and I loved him to death.

Our home in the country was a quiet, peaceful place surrounded by cornfields. There were good memories in our Skyline home, and all of us were so happy at first. But as nice as it was, it didn't last long. It was just the beginning of the end for our family—before it broke to pieces all around us.

My parents' marriage was on the rocks, and one day when I was about ten years old, the tension building in our lives snapped our home apart like a worn-out spring. It was morning, and we were home with Mom and her "new friend," a man she seemed pretty friendly with. He was an acquaintance of my dad's. Dad had introduced Mom to him so the guy could do some maintenance work around the house when my dad was on duty. Mom smelt of vodka and cigarettes. She was rummaging through her purse to find us change for lunch money and making sure our hair and teeth were brushed and our clothes matched. But she was not in good shape.

I looked out the window and saw the squad car coming down the driveway, and I thought to myself, *This is gonna be bad.* My dad got out of the squad car and had his .44 Magnum—like Clint Eastwood's—already pulled out of its holster. He saw me in the window and gave me a look that said, "Don't say a thing." He snuck through the garage and slammed through the cracked-open side door into the kitchen. He nearly kicked the door right off the hinges.

My mother and her "friend" panicked. The new guy fell on all fours. He started crawling to the door, but my dad grabbed him and slammed him against the wall.

"I trusted you to be around my family, and you're out here stealing my wife! I'll blow your fucking head off, you motherfucker!

The man pled with Dad, trembling and holding up his hands. "The kids are here! The kids are here!"

Dad had a way of looking at you that made the bottom of your stomach drop—a real "Oh, Shit!" moment. Dad's eyes met mine, and he pointed to the back of the house. I knew what that meant. My brother and I ran to our room and shut the door, but we saw enough before we got there, and we heard everything.

"You stay away from my wife!" Dad yelled, and he kicked the guy in the ass. Mom's "friend" crawled out the door. Then Dad turned around to yell at Mom.

My brother, Tim, peeked out the bedroom door to see what was happening. "We've gotta go, or we'll miss the bus!"

"Lemme look!" I said.

I crept to the front of the house and saw the bus coming down the road. I yelled at Tim to hurry, and we snuck out the front door and ran a short distance along the front of our property to the bus stop. As I climbed on, I looked over my shoulder to the rear of our property. Dad, in his full police uniform, had the man up against the side of the barn behind the house, and Dad was screaming, "You're fucking trying to steal my wife!" in full view of everyone onboard the bus.

Inside the bus, it was dead silent. All the kids were glued to the windows watching the drama unfold, and then they turned and saw me and my brother. Nobody said anything. Then, a kid from my class broke the silence. "Jimmy was that—?" But that was all he got out of his mouth before I leaped over the seat and beat the hell out of him. I was so angry. My perfect life was unraveling, and I couldn't do anything about it.

When we arrived at school, a furious, painful knot had formed in my empty, hungry stomach. Going to school where I did was an unfulfilling and dangerous experience. Our school boundaries had the highest crime and unemployment rate in the country. Most inner-city schools had a pecking order or turf that a certain clique claimed, and it was no different at my school. The bathroom we called "front bathroom" was one of those places.

I was only in fifth grade, but I didn't take any shit from anyone. I went into the front bathroom to wash up and calm down after beating in the face of the kid on the school bus. If I didn't hurry, I wouldn't make it to class. I was a White kid, and everyone knew White kids didn't go near that front bathroom. It was the Black kids' turf, and if they found you in there, they would make sure you didn't come out until *someone* was bleeding or knocked out. I didn't care. Nothing scared me. I just needed to clean up.

As I was washing my hands, an older Black kid came out of one of the stalls and spotted me. His name was Joe Joe. I didn't know him that well, but his brother was a good friend of mine. Apparently, Joe Joe didn't know that. He strutted over and sat right in front of me on the sink I was trying to use. Then he started to pick out his afro in the mirror to make it as big as he could. That was the trend back then. The Black guys had huge afros and kept picks stuck in their hair, and the White guys kept their hair long and feathered. It took a lot of maintenance to look cool.

Joe Joe started to taunt me. "Man, I hear you're like the baddest cat alive. Real tough. I want to try you sometime, man."

I was in no mood for this shit after the way my day had started. I wasn't going to put up with it for long. "Dude, get out of my way. I'm trying to get out of here and get to class," I said, meeting his gaze firmly in the mirror.

Joe Joe hauled off and hit me square in the face, and I don't remember much after that. When I finished beating the shit out of him, I put his head in the toilet to cool it off. Near the end, his brother came through the door and saw his brother lying on the floor and beaten to a pulp.

"Man, Jimmy, whatcha doing to my brother?"

"James, don't make me get on you next, man. Your brother started this shit, and I ended it."

James walked over, bent down, and slapped his brother in the face. Joe Joe groggily raised his head. "You know, you don't fuck with Jimmy Keene, man," James said. "What's wrong with you?"

When I turned around, the bathroom had filled with Black students. It seemed like at least a hundred had gathered to see what had caused the ruckus. I walked toward the door, and the throng silently parted like the red sea. I could see my brother at the back of the crowd.

Back in the hall, my brother fell into step beside me and asked what happened. Judging by his blood-drained expression, he hadn't been sure I'd come out alive. He exhaled with relief, and we headed to our classes.

My mom continued to see her new "friend." It should have stopped then, but it didn't. We had to endure a few more drives with my dad in his squad car looking for Mom so he could go to work. Eventually, Mom and Dad decided it would be better to split up. My mother admitted later in life that she had made a mistake divorcing Dad. Even though things were rocky, he took care of her the best he could, and he did far better than the loser that became my stepdad.

Mom tried, too, but she lived a hard life. I liked to show her love and appreciation whenever I could. She and Dad were so busy that neither of them got to enjoy a lot of nice things. One day during the spring, I was riding my bike home from a friend's house and noticed a field full of wildflowers. Hell, some may have actually been weeds, but I thought they were beautiful. I pulled over, jumped the fence, and picked a variety of blooms, thinking I would surprise my mom with them. When I got home, she was getting ready for work.

"Mom, these are for you," I said, presenting the bouquet. She froze, her eyes wide with surprise and shock. Then she started to cry.

"Thank you, Jimmy." This is the nicest thing anyone has done for me in a long time. You're my sweet boy." She smiled at me, and my core swelled with a rare feeling of warmth and love.

Years later, after my mom had passed, I was cleaning out old belongings and came across my baby book. It wasn't large, but it was heartwarming to see it after all those years. It included baby pictures of my early years and listed milestones—nothing apart from the ordinary expected material. But when I flipped to the back, I was dumbfounded to find the handful of wildflowers I had picked for my mom when I was young all pressed between the pages. I remembered them instantly.

"Mom, you kept these?" I said out loud as if she were still there to hear me. "I can't believe it. They weren't anything special. I just picked them out of a field."

But I recalled how much those flowers had meant to her and her heartfelt words to me: "Jimmy, these flowers just made my day. I will never ever throw them away. It was such a sweet thought, and that's what counts. I'll always save them." The evidence that she had done just that lay right before my eyes years later. I can't express how deeply that touched me and still does whenever I think about it.

I realized then that even though we didn't spend as much time with our mom as kids that had stay-at-home moms to cook and clean and do the laundry, our mom loved us just as much. Life was never easy, but Mom had a huge heart, and she was always willing to help a friend or family member in any way she could.

After that morning Dad came home early, my family's happy moments all together dwindled to nothing. Mom eventually married the new guy and supported him along with us kids. My wonderful dad was gone and out of the house forever, and I became a pissed-off kid in general. Mom and our stepdad spent every single night at the bar restaurant my mom eventually owned. It had a little house in back, so she stayed there with her new husband most of the time working and drinking.

We basically had no parental supervision starting at the ages of ten, eight, and five. No one was ever home at the Skyline house except us kids. The statistics for a child with no father in the home winding up in prison are staggering. Add our absentee mother and our high-crime, high-unemployment environment, and it was a perfect cocktail to end up on a wayward path. I took out my rage on the street and on the sports field. My parents weren't perfect, but I loved them, and they did all they could with what they had at the time. But the hardships in my childhood didn't end there.

CHAPTER 2

NEARLY SUPERMAN

My father was everything to me. Even though he was forced out of his home and not present as much as we grew up, in my eyes, he was Superman. I wasn't the only person who loved my father. Our community and his co-workers loved and respected him just as much as I did. My dad was a big guy. He stood six-foot-five and weighed three hundred pounds, but he was all muscle. If you weren't intimidated by his presence, then you were either crazy or a fool. My dad was charming and charismatic. Everywhere he went, people buzzed around him, and women loved to see him in his uniform.

My father saved countless lives during his impressive twenty-three-year career as a police officer and twenty-four years as a fireman. He loved to be in the heat of the action and was the first to raise his hand for the most dangerous assignments. Sometimes people would call him for help just because of his powerful appearance.

One day when I was a kid, Dad and I had just left football practice, and he had to swing by the police station for something. When we walked in, one of the sergeants on duty saw him and called him over.

"Oh God, Jim, I'm so glad to see you today!" I could hear raucous yelling and banging in the back of the station coming from the direction of the holding cells.

"Who do you have up there making all that noise?" Dad asked.

"It's Choo-Choo again, and he's really in one of his moods! Nobody can shut him the fuck up! He's threatening to beat up anyone that gets close enough, and he's already tried it. Steve was wrestling Choo-Choo into the cell to sober him up, and he hit Steve in the face! It really ticked Steve off. I swear he was going to kill Choo-Choo over it. Can you work some of your magic please?"

I followed my dad upstairs to the jail cells and could smell the alcohol thirty feet from where the man was. Choo-Choo was a huge Black man about my dad's size, and he seemed like a pretty crazy, out-of-control dude. Clearly, he was homeless and enraged. He reeked of booze and body odor. I didn't want to get any closer. But my dad went right up to the cell bars.

"Hey, Choo-Choo! How're you doin' today?"

"Oh hi, Officer Keene. Ahhhhh! My head is pounding out of control, and these assholes won't shut up or give me anything to eat! It's really pissing me off!"

"That's too bad. Listen, Choo-Choo—you can't act like this here. If I got you a sandwich, could you take it easy 'til they release you? I really don't want to come in there, because it won't be good for you." Dad said that last bit casually, but Choo-Choo's eyes snapped up to attention, and he sat down on the bench.

"Yeah, man. No problem. I—I don't want no problems with you, Officer Keene. Don't want *any* trouble with you."

"*That* is why we love your dad," Dad's coworker said a little while later, patting my back as we left the police station. "Your dad has a talent for diffusing or physically handling difficult situations unlike anyone I've ever seen. He's the best at what he does!" I didn't know it then, but I had inherited those same skills, and my dad encouraged me to develop them. They would prove invaluable to me in the years ahead.

Our home on Skyline was on top of a big hill, and because it was located on the back roads, people thought they could travel around the area with no regard for the speed limit at all. The problem was that when you were driving over the hill, you couldn't see if something was in front of you until it was too late to avoid it. When we waited for our bus in the morning,

Dad would yell at us to get away from the road and back up. The danger the road presented really concerned him. He bought a large tool shed and set it up fifteen feet away from the road and put a bench inside. Then he found two huge boulders and put one on each side of the shed. Dad said that setup would help if a car were to lose control over the rise of the hill. The car would hit the boulders, and they would take the brunt of the force and keep the car from hitting the shed.

It was so cool to have our own sheltered bus stop outside our house. Soon, all the neighborhood kids came to our stop to catch the bus even if it was out of their way—especially on cold, wet days. Some parents would even drop their kids off there instead of using the stops closer to their homes.

One of those days, a kid named Dean was messing around in front of the gathered group, shaking his butt and doing goofy dances. He would dodge into the street and then back over to us and then back to the street to see if the bus was coming. At one point, he turned around to say something to us, and a car full of teenagers came over the hill at eighty miles per hour and didn't see Dean in the road. They hit him so hard that he flew as high as the treetops. As he fell back down, he was hit again by another car coming the other direction. It happened so fast, we all watched in total silence, unable to comprehend it.

The little group of onlooking kids was stunned into stillness. I finally gathered my wits and ran over to the ditch where Dean had landed. He had blood gushing out of his head in sickening spurts that matched the beat of his heart. Blood came out of his mouth in sputters while he tried to catch his breath and speak.

"Help me! Help me—please!"

I ran as fast as I could, yelling for my dad all the way up our driveway. I was halfway to the house when Dad came out of the front door, still doing up his pants and shoving one arm into a sleeve.

"Jimmy! What's wrong?"

He could tell by the look on my face and the silent kids behind me that something terrible had happened—all of our eyes were as big as saucers. I turned around and ran back to where Dean was lying. Dad was right on my heels. I stopped short of the ditch, but Dad followed my gaze and ran ahead to crouch next to Dean.

"Help me!"

"Don't speak, son." As my dad soothed Dean's panic, he quickly assessed the boy's injuries. Then he stood up and walked urgently back to my side. "Jimmy, this kid is in bad condition," he said in a low voice. "He's not going to make it unless you do exactly what I ask. I need you to go out to the barn and get one of those big boards I've been using to build the shelves out there. Run and get it here—fast. Timmy, go help your brother—GO!"

We dashed to the barn, our hearts pounding in our throats, and found the board Dad wanted. When we returned, Dad was doing everything he could to slow Dean's bleeding and keep him stable. Then, Dad calmly moved Dean onto the board with professional skill, loaded him in the back of my mom's big Cadillac, and drove him to the hospital. When Dad arrived, the doctors were amazed that his makeshift medical treatments had kept Dean alive.

Almost half the bones in Dean's body were crushed, his skull had caved in, and he had multiple internal injuries. It took several surgeries throughout Dean's school years and into his adult life to repair the damage, but he survived. He was always grateful that my dad had been there to stabilize him and take him to the hospital. Dad's swift action saved Dean's life.

Dad always did that sort of thing. Saving people in trouble was part of who he was. He had a particular knack for handling difficult situations and staying cool under pressure. Helping and serving others was a big part of his career too, but that's not the only reason he did what he did—he was just good at it, and he never passed up an opportunity to help whether he was on duty or not.

Another time, Dad made it into the paper. While he was driving home from work, he passed a burning house. Smoke billowed from the roof, and the house's interior was engulfed in a flaming inferno. There was a woman on the sidewalk weeping and crying for her daughter who was still inside. Dad didn't think twice before running into the building with no special gear. The girl's muffled cries led my dad through the suffocating smoke, and he found her hiding in the closet. He brought her out of the fire to the ambulance just as a photographer snapped his picture. It was in the paper the next day. Sadly, several firemen perished that day in that fire, but the little girl survived.

My dad had a long career, but it slowed down after a dangerous police raid one night at a late-night, after-hours gin distillery and gambling house in a high-crime-ridden district of south Chicago. Dad and his team showed up at the shady business at 3 a.m. in full tactical gear, a search warrant in hand. The team split into two units, one for the front entrance and one for the back entrance. Dad's group went to the back, and the only back entrance was on the second floor. Since my dad was big, he was always the first to go through the door with the battering ram or his own shoulder. When he hit the door, it exploded, and the deafening shockwave slammed into him—the door had been boobytrapped. The blast blew Dad off the second floor and sent him hurtling to the ground below. He broke his back when he landed—a complete break, clean through the spine.

Paramedics rushed him to the hospital and put him in traction. He had emergency surgery, and we were told he might never walk again, but Dad couldn't be brought down so easily. The surgery was a success, and he did walk again. He lost more than an inch of his height, and he went through years of rehab and eventually a second back surgery, but he did better than his doctors anticipated. However, his spirit was never quite the same again. He was no longer eager to be in the thick of the action. He mainly worked inside the police station and not so much out on the streets anymore. He retired two years later. A year after that, he retired from the fire department too. His injury had taken the wind out of his sail.

My dad was also a championship pool player—the best I've seen even to this day. When Dad was only a year into his police career, the department had budget cuts, so they laid off the new guys—including my dad. Dad made a living playing professional pool for two years until the layoff ended. He taught my brother and me to play at a young age. Growing up and as adults, we always owned a pool table and hung out at pool halls so we could play each other and any other sucker we came across who thought he could beat one of us.

We both got really good but never could master the art like Dad.

While Dad was recovering from his injury, he got to the point he could do some work, so he took a private security job for a warehouse in Indiana, just over the state line. Graveyard shift was always the newbie's responsibility, but Dad didn't mind because it got him back on his feet walking around and nursing his back injury without too much strain. One early morning, as he drove home in the darkness just before dawn, he still had his .44 Magnum concealed under his jacket. As he settled in for the ride, he saw a guy stumble out of the tree-lined back country roads. He looked injured. Ahead of him was a rusty green station wagon that was pulled over with its emergency lights on.

Dad was driving his black, mint-condition El Camino with Cragars and sixties. That vehicle was the talk of the town in those days. He always had fancy, souped-up cars in the driveway that all the guys would drool over, mainly Corvettes. The man flagged Dad down, and he pulled off the road to see if he could help. He got out and approached the guy, but the man suddenly pulled a sawed-off shotgun out of his long jacket and stuck it right in my dad's side.

"Let's go," he growled in Dad's ear. "I want you to walk slowly back to your car and open the passenger door."

Dad did what he was told, but he was already looking for an opportunity to take the guy down. Unfortunately, the bastard slid in right behind him on the bench seat of the car, and the gun never left Dad's side.

"Start driving," the man said, his eyes darting from side to side. Dad obeyed. About a mile up the road, he told Dad to pull over. "Give me the keys and open your door slowly." He didn't allow Dad any chance to turn the tables—the gun jammed into Dad's ribs so tight it began to break his skin. As they walked around the car, three more guys jumped out of a close-by ditch and grabbed Dad. They threw him down into the ditch they just came from where another hostage was already lying face down with his hands above his head.

"Man, we need to kill them. They've seen our faces. No witnesses," said a tall, lanky man in dirty clothes who smelled of engine oil.

"Let's just get out of here. Look at that car! Man, it's a beauty."

After twenty minutes of arguing about whether to kill their hostages, the men finally decided to leave. They piled into Dad's car. As the doors closed, Dad popped up out of the ditch, aimed his .44 Magnum at the car, and fired several rounds into the bad-ass El Camino's body. I would have loved to see the looks on those dudes' faces when they realized my dad had a gun on him that whole time! But they got away.

Dad checked on the other guy in the ditch, and they made their way to a nearby farmhouse where he called the police department in Kankakee. They put out an APB for my dad's car. The funny thing is, when the car crossed the border into Illinois, the men drove right into Kankakee. Dad's fellow officers at the department spotted them immediately and easily apprehended them.

All of the men were prior convicts and murderers. It was a good day's work to be able to get them off the street, and Dad was glad to get his car back, even with a few bullet holes in it.

When Dad's health finally forced him to slow down, he lost everything financially. One time, I was in town from Chicago visiting friends and family and decided to go over to my dad's place to say "Hi." When I arrived, I found a handful of deputies from the sheriff's office standing outside. I went up to the man that seemed to be in charge and asked what was going on. I recognized him immediately as a kid a grew up with on Elm Street. His dad was a cop back then with my dad.

"Hey, Adam. It's been a while. What's going on?"

"Hey, Jimmy. I have another eviction notice here for your dad. He's ignored all of the previous notices. He really needs to get out of the house today. I know he's in there, and I need to arrest him." He looked at me like he would rather be doing anything other than that right then.

"I've got keys. Let me go take a look." As I walked around to the side of the house and opened the door, I could see Dad crouching by the window and peering outside.

"Jimmy, these assholes are trying to take my house. I can't lose this, too!" At that moment, I realized my dad was really hurting. I wanted to help him and make him happy. I was doing well for myself financially and wanted to take some of the pressure off. I went outside and told Adam that Dad wasn't in the house and that I had looked everywhere. They left, but I knew they'd be back. I went back inside and found Dad where I'd left him.

"Dad, what's going on? Why are they trying to evict you?"

"Oh, the last year's been so hard with the surgeries and rehab on my back. The owners knew all that and knew I was gonna pay them. I can't believe they're doing this to me!"

"Give me their names and number so I can call them and try to sort this out."

This wasn't the first time Dad had dealt with getting kicked off property he couldn't pay for. The year before, he'd had to file for bankruptcy and almost lost a house he'd bought on the river. I helped him out so he could keep it. The house was hardly habitable, but it was prime real estate, and Dad had big dreams of turning it into a restaurant and gas station. He'd hung his hopes on using income from the restaurant to pay for the house he was living in.

Later that night, I called the owners of his current home to speak with them. A man answered the phone. He told me that Dad had entered a rent-to-own agreement, but he hadn't paid anything for almost a year, and they couldn't allow him to live there any longer. The house was worth just under a million dollars and at that time had another ten acres attached to it, making it worth around 1.6 million. My dad's pension from the police and his civil work was only around nine hundred dollars a month, and I knew his trucking business wasn't making much. His restaurant plans with the house on the river hadn't materialized.

But my dad was my dad. I asked the owner to meet me at my bank the following morning, and just before we walked through the bank's front door the next day, I handed Dad the money. He immediately stood at attention, straightened his posture, and came back to life. Seeing that made me feel like all was right in the world again. We paid cash for the house. The owners were relieved, and Dad was elated.

"Dad, I want you to please hold onto the title for Tim and me so that we'll have a house in the neighborhood later on that stays in the family." And he promised. Before I left town, I bought him a new Corvette, because his car had been repossessed, a new Harley Davidson motorcycle, and eventually a new Chevy 4x4.

I knew it would make him happy and thought if those were paid off, then he wouldn't have to worry about making payments. He could just enjoy living his life and be the proud man I had always known him to be.

Dad didn't know what I was up to. At some point, he asked me how I was coming up with so much money, and I told him I was working at the stock market in Chicago and raking in millions. Many people have become very rich working at the Chicago stock market, so it wasn't an unbelievable story. He didn't question me further. He had to ask, but I got the feeling he didn't really want to know.

If I'd told him the truth, I knew he would've been disappointed. It would've been a big conflict with him being a retired cop. I think he wondered deep down, but he turned a blind eye because he loved me.

I helped Dad financially a lot over the years, but he struggled to capitalize on the funds I provided for all of his business ventures. He reminded me of Ralph Kramden from the *Honeymooners*—he always had big, ingenious ideas, but no matter how good they looked at the start, they all turned sour and failed. The first business I bought him was a trucking business. He really loved trucking, and it never fully failed, but it was a hard business and never soared either. He did enjoy it, though.

Then, on Dad's advice, I bought an Italian food business called Gusto Italian Foods. There was a fancy upscale restaurant and a frozen-food manufacturing plant to go with the purchase. The deal also included distribution contracts for established frozen-food items in major grocery stores. I invested an initial four million and eventually two million more over the next several years. We even had a board of investors including Walter Payton and Matt Suhey of the Chicago Bears. I left the business in Dad's control—it was his baby to sink or soar. Gusto was up and flying and showed great promise until it eventually crashed and burned. Both Matt Suhey and Walter Payton bailed out halfway through our ownership period, and Matt Suhey started American Water, a bottled water company. I wished I had gone into bottled water instead.

On another occasion, my dad talked me into flying down to Texas to hear a pitch on oil wells. We ended up buying them, but it turned into the same old story. The wells looked good, and the numbers looked good, but they barely produced any oil at all. Once again—a failed business and a major financial loss. It was hard on Dad to watch his dreams go up in smoke time after time. He was a proud and strong man, but each time he felt that he'd failed, he lost some of that steam and strength.

Dad wasn't perfect, but he was everything to me, and I loved him. What he lacked in financial success, he made up for by helping other people. His life included more stories of bravery and courage than I could ever have time to tell! Whenever we were together in public, strangers would say kind words like, "Thank you for your service." My family got accustomed to it back then and didn't think much of it, but after reflecting on it, I realized just how special that acknowledgment was.

The number of people Dad helped especially hit home after he passed away. When our family arrived at the funeral home, the parking lot was full, and the street on both sides and around the block as far as the eye could see was full of cars. There were two sets of family—my mother and us kids and his present wife. It was a little awkward because Mom took the traditional position of the wife with us at her side. I didn't miss the dirty look from his new wife, but my mother didn't pay any attention to her. We were there early, but the halls were full of people, and they poured into the viewing room. One by one, they offered their condolences and shared stories with us about Dad, some in tears, others more composed.

"I worked with Big Jim for ten years. I would never want anyone but your dad on my six. He had everyone's back and always came in at 110 percent. He never made stupid moves. He was an amazing officer."

Dean was there with his family. I hadn't seen him since we were in school together. When he finally got to the casket, I could see a tear in his eye.

"Hey, Jimmy! Good to see you! I'm sorry about your dad's passing."

"Hey, Dean! Man, we've grown up!" We laughed. Dean looked good, but he still bore scars. When I saw them, I felt a pit form in my stomach, and the day of his accident flashed before my eyes.

"Your dad saved my life, you know. I wouldn't be here if it weren't for him." He wiped another tear away. He gave me a hug and walked on.

Swarms of people came through that line, all with some story about my dad. Hours passed with no end in sight. The funeral director had to extend the viewing hours as we waited for the line to diminish. Many people stayed until the end, chatting with each other and catching up.

When it was finally time to drive to the cemetery, we all loaded into the car. There were several vehicles carrying extended family, and ours was right behind the hearse. As we pulled into the street, both sides were lined with police cruisers, firetrucks, police officers, and firefighters for as far as the eye could see. All the officers and firefighters wore full dress uniforms and saluted as we passed. During the long drive, each underpass we traveled under was full of people. We passed people paying respects for the full forty-five-minute drive to the grave.

I will never forget that day. I felt so proud of who my father was and what he meant to not only me and my family but also to so many others in our communities of Kankakee and Chicago. When they laid his casket down in the ground, I felt something break in my heart. My dad, my hero—Superman—was really gone, and my life would never be the same. I would forever have an empty spot where he had been.

CHAPTER 3

WELCOME TO FUCKING POVERTY

When a couple got divorced back then, the mother usually got to keep the house and raise the kids there. Being the oldest, I was asked by my mom's lawyer to say which parent I wanted to live with. I was only ten. I didn't understand why any of this shit was happening. My brother was nine, and my sister was three and a half.

I'll never forget arriving at the court that day; my dad caught us all in the hallway, and he pulled me to the side and said, "Son, listen—I'm not gonna be mad at you if you tell the court that you want to live with your mom. I think the best place for you is to be out at the house on Skyline in the country with the rest of the family." He grabbed me and hugged me tightly. I saw tears in his eyes, and I had to choke down the frog in my throat.

That choice was difficult. I loved my dad. I didn't understand why my dad had left our house. We went into the proceeding, and I was put on the stand. The judge asked me who I wanted to live with as my dad sat to the right, and my mom sat to the left. I looked at Dad, and I could see more tears welling up in his eyes. He smiled and nodded his head. I looked at Mom, and I said, "I wanna live with my mom." It broke my heart, even if I did have Dad's approval.

Things certainly didn't get easier after that. It was like someone from the government showered us with a pitiful handful of confetti and said, "Congratulations! You've been awarded twenty dollars per child from the state of Illinois for child support. Welcome to fucking poverty!"

The divorce was pretty ugly. My father was forced to leave the home that he'd paid for. He moved to the far west side of Kankakee forty-five minutes away, so he wasn't there to pick up the slack. My mother had to work even harder, and—of course—she still stayed out well into the next day, and she left us alone a lot. Her loser boyfriend—soon-to-be stepdad—wasn't much help. He moved in but never helped financially or with raising us. The man never really had a job. He was there to answer to Mom's every beck and call and do anything she wanted. Over the years, she treated him like shit. I almost felt sorry for the guy, but it never overtook my anger at him for breaking up my family.

Mom tried to compensate by having babysitters help us as much as she could afford, but that wasn't often. One such babysitter named Susie was my favorite. She was sixteen. She never made me feel like a child. At ten, I felt I was old enough not to need a babysitter, but I never minded when she came over. Susie had long brown hair styled like Farrah Fawcett. It lay around her face and framed it perfectly. She always smelled of bubble gum or cotton candy and carried her flavored lip gloss all the time, applying it frequently. She also wore tightly fitting T-shirts that showed off what was underneath. Being around her was the first time I was aware of having physical feelings toward girls. When she bent down to give me a hug before she left, I could look down and see exactly what she held against me as she wrapped her arms around me.

Most of the time when she came over, she would make us dinner. That was always a treat even if it was out of a can or a box. She made sure we did our homework, bathed, and got ready for bed at a decent time.

One night she was on the phone for an hour and seemed really distracted. She rushed us to bed thirty minutes early, and a little while later, I heard a soft knock on the door and whispers coming from the front room. I snuck into the hall to see what was going on.

There was a tall boy there with her, and they were arguing.

"Come on, Susie, they won't even know. We can have some fun. I brought the beer!"

"Kenny, I can't. I told you. You're going to wake them up."

"I drove all the way across town to the middle of nowhere to spend time with you alone and in private. The least you can do is kiss me."

"I said no! I need this job." Kenny grabbed her hands and pulled her toward the couch. Susie pulled back. "Ouch! Let go! That hurts, you brute!"

That's all it took. I burst out of the hallway at full speed and tried to tackle Kenny. I started slugging him and kicking him as hard as I could.

"Get the fuck out of my house!" I screamed. "My dad is a cop! Get away from her, you asshole!"

Kenny was pretty good at keeping his vitals covered and dodging my attacks. "Hey, kid, that hurts! I'm not hurting anyone. Tell him."

Susie looked at Kenny and rolled her eyes. "Jimmy, he wasn't hurting me, but Kenny, you need to leave now!" Susie pulled me to her side, and we both escorted Kenny to the door. When we shut the door with him on the other side, Susie grabbed me and said, "Thanks, little man! That was really nice of you to protect me." She gave me a kiss on the cheek. "Now get to bed. It's late!"

That night when I went back to my room, all I could think about was that kiss. It was the first time I realized that girls liked a strong man to protect them and provide for them. This became a well-rounded trait later in my life and affected my relationships with women.

I ran into Susie years later. I was probably twenty at the time and spending a lot of time in the VIP section of some of the hottest nightclubs in downtown Chi-Town. One night the VIP waitress leaned down to pick up our glasses and smiled at me. I knew her instantly. Susie had matured into a gorgeous woman.

"Susie, is that you?" I asked, looking her up and down.

"I haven't been called that in ages. Shit, Jimmy Keene, is that you?"

"Yeah, it's me. All grown up!"

"Damn, you sure did! Look at you. I always knew you would be a lady killer when you grew up, but damn!"

We caught up and chatted each time she would bring us drinks, and we both felt a strong connection. She told me she remembered that night with Kenny and was so impressed by how I had stood up for her. She said no one had ever done that for her before and that I had been such a little gentleman. I waited for her to get off work and invited her back to the brownstone for an after-party. We hung out for a few more months, and it was amazing. Running into your childhood crush is something to remember.

My dad taught me to respect women and treat them like ladies at an early age. He would always pull out their chairs, open their car doors, give them compliments, and tell them they were beautiful. The apple didn't fall far from the tree. I found that a woman placed more value on respect than on a quick fuck and that a sincere compliment would soften the heart. I learned that if I acknowledged a woman's needs in bed and put her desires before my own, she would almost always invite me back for more.

It didn't take long before Mom couldn't afford Susie, and Susie really needed the money and wasn't able to do it for free. I was sad to see her leave. It got pretty bad when we were left on our own. One day my brother, Timmy, and I had an all-out war over who got the hot-dog and the last two pieces of bacon in the fridge. We beat each other bloody with our fists over it.

I decided to confront Mom about our circumstances. I was tired of not having any food in the house, and I had holes in my sneakers.

Mom had just gotten up and was ratting her hair high and putting on her makeup in front of her mirror. It probably wasn't my best idea to talk to her about such a testy subject that early because she would usually wake up as grumpy as a bear. I brought my siblings with me for support. How could she deny all of us?

"Mom, I really need some money, please. I know you've been working really hard, but Timmy needs some new pants without holes in them, and one of my sneakers has a hole in the sole. Just give it to me, and I'll go to the store, so you don't have to worry about it."

Mom stopped applying her eyeliner mid-stroke and met my gaze in the reflection. I couldn't read her expression as her eyes flicked from me to Timmy and then to my little sister running around the room. Her tired expression morphed into hurt and then into anger. Then her fury exploded.

"I DON'T HAVE ANY FUCKING MONEY!" she screamed. We all ran back to our room and closed the door. When I turned around, my siblings' wide, tear-filled eyes were locked on me.

"Jimmy, I'm hungry," Timmy said. "And I really need some new pants. The kids are making fun of me behind my back."

Terri nodded. "I'm hungry, too, Jimmy."

Her small face looked so dejected and resigned to her gnawing hunger, that I couldn't bear it. I knew I had to do something because no help was coming from anywhere else. After the highly emotional divorce, I had effectively lost my childhood. I had to focus on supporting my siblings and myself. I knew if I wanted to get the new sneakers I needed for track or a new Walkman like the other kids were bragging about having, I had to do something myself to make it happen.

I started out with a paper route, and I made sure the papers were delivered on time and weren't thrown in the bushes to get the best tips. I detasseled corn, and I walked beans. "Walking beans" is when you walk along the bean rows with a small cutting instrument and chop all the weeds out of the beans. It was a rough gig. My fingers bled, and I had blisters on every part of my hands. But that didn't stop me even though the pay was next to nothing. At ten years old, it's not like you have a lot of job opportunities knocking at your door. Later on, I worked at the gun club setting traps for the shooters. On my days off I would spend hours learning how to shoot all types of guns and I really enjoyed it. I soon became a marksman. I also worked at the local gas station. I did everything I could think of to make money.

One day during early spring, Timmy and my best friends Richie O'Reilly, Robbie, and Kev-C were hanging out, riding our bikes, and getting into whatever other trouble we could. We rode our bikes down one of the back roads, with green corn fields stretching for miles on both sides of the street. I suddenly spotted a big, dark green lump that looked out of place tucked nearly out of sight several rows of corn back and thought, *What the hell? Let's go see what it is.*

"Hey, guys, wait up. I see something."

"Man, I gotta get home before dark, or my mom is gonna kill me."

"Stop being a pussy, Richie. It won't take long. Maybe it's a dead body!" I punched his arm and started laughing as I ran toward the lump.

When we got closer, we saw that the lump was comprised of several large garbage bags very full of something. We all looked at each other, and I walked over and opened the top one. A pungent smell came wafting out. Living where we did, we all knew what that smell was even by the tender age of ten—marijuana.

Richie yelled, "Holy shit! Look at all that weed."

"Leave it alone." I walked around looking for traces of who the hell had left it there and whether they were close by.

"Man, we could smoke this until we graduated and still have leftovers!" Richie said, opening the second bag.

"My brother would buy some for himself. He loves this shit," Kev-C added.

And then my mind started to spin. *What if we could sell it? There's enough here for everyone we know and more. How much money would we make?*

"Guys, no one leaves this much weed in a cornfield without planning to come back and get it. And I don't wanna be here when they do. Let's pull it further back into the field so no one will come across it easily, and if it's here in a few weeks, it's ours."

That night, I couldn't fall asleep. All I could think about was whether someone would claim that marijuana prize in the cornfield. My entrepreneurial instincts started kicking in.

Every week for the next seven months, one of us visited the field, and all the bags of marijuana stayed where we left them. The cornstalks would be cut soon.

If we wanted to take the bags, it had to be before then. So late one night by the light of the full moon, we went and gathered the bags hidden in the desolate stretch of farmland. None of us realized how those giant bags would change the rest of our lives.

With our lack of parental supervision and a big barn in our yard, we had no problem storing the weed undetected and dividing it for sale. I knew the older fifteen-to-seventeen-year-old kids in town, and I approached them with our new goods, and the weed flew out faster than we could pack it up in little bags. Homegrown weed over seven months old isn't anything spectacular, but everyone wanted some, and we got rich.

We kept selling that haul of marijuana for three years. That weed distribution phase I started piqued the interest of a Mexican dealer named Jose on the south side of Chicago who wanted to know why his inventory wasn't moving the same as before. The dealer heard about me and my crew and wanted to meet me in person. I was about thirteen years old by then, and I'm sure he was surprised when a cocky kid walked in to meet with a Mexican drug lord. He looked me up and down, scratching his chin.

"Are you responsible for my lagging weed sales in south Chicago and Kankakee?"

"Yeah, and?" I didn't flinch.

He continued to stare at me, like he was making his mind up about something. "How old are you, kid?"

"Fifteen," I lied.

"You're younger than I expected, moving that much in the big sections of Kankakee and south Chicago like you have been. Where you gettin' your supply?"

"None of your business." I looked right back at him.

Jose laughed like a thunderclap. I had no idea what he was laughing about.

"I like you, kid. You got big balls and swagger! I want you to work for me. I'll supply you with as much weed as you can handle—you just can't buy from anyone else. What do you think?"

"All right. You have yourself a deal."

Now, this Mexican, pure-grade weed was something else compared to the homegrown stuff, and we couldn't keep enough coming in to handle the demand. I needed a bigger crew. We expanded to supply all the parties kids were having for miles around.

I tended to my money like I would never see another dollar again. I took care of the family and bought the clothes and shoes my siblings and I needed, but I hid most of the cash in the rafters of our barn. Nobody else really went in there, and it was hidden well enough and far enough out of easy reach that no one could ever find it. Life changed for us. Eventually, I was making more than my dad's yearly civil-duty wage, then more than both my parents made together in a year of Mom busting her back and Dad putting his life in danger daily with criminals on the street. I swore at that time that I would never feel the pangs of hunger in my belly again, and now I had the resources to make that happen. Poverty would be a thing of the past.

As I got older, my business developed right along with me. When my friends needed extra money, they would help me move my product here and there. The business grew faster than I ever imagined. My life had turned into a whirlwind. Between sports practices and games, dealing with my new enterprise, and the constant girlfriends I was dating, there was little time for schoolwork. But grades weren't a problem for me. I was always an A and B student and able to keep grades up along with everything else.

In high school, I still put a lot of effort into sports. Dad was busy with his new wife, and I didn't see him much, but he made a point to never miss any of my football games. He wholeheartedly felt I had the potential to play professionally, and my coaches and everyone else thought I could, too. When I saw him watching in the stands, I wanted to play my best so I could see his big smile and hear him say, "You played an amazing game, son." It felt like his praise and encouragement gave me superhuman strength, and I played even better as a result.

I lettered in three sports each year, and I had four scholarships to choose from during my senior year. All of those offers were from out-of-state universities, and all were too far for me to attend while still managing my growing empire.

You may want to say, "Okay, Jimmy, you've made it. You have a full scholarship. Get out of the marijuana business and go to the big university." That's what many kids dream of, right? To play college ball in a big-ten program, have a free ride, and possibly go pro? But it's not exactly free. Sure, they pay for your tuition, but if you attend school, you still have to pay for housing expenses and other costs. If I had traveled far away from my business, I wouldn't have had the money for that. I also had a younger brother and sister at home to look after, who really needed my help. It was a hard decision, but I stayed in Chicago and attended a local college so I could still manage the marijuana sales. I continued to wrestle and play football on my local college's nationally ranked teams until after my sophomore year. I always stayed involved in martial arts, and I've continued that my whole life. I was still young and felt I could do anything. The money was just too good to walk away from. It was completely intoxicating.

When I was seventeen, Mom sat me down and told me that as soon as I graduated, I had to move out. She'd always warned us that we had to leave the house at seventeen. She couldn't afford to support me any longer, and I would be on my own. At first, it terrified me. Where would I go? I didn't *have* anywhere to go. Dad's house was full, and I didn't feel welcome there with his new family. I found out about a wrestling house near the college that had a spare room. "Room" was not the best term for some of the living arrangements. A few of the bedrooms were literally closets that someone had walled in to offer a little privacy. They'd even put a board up and called it a door. But all I needed was a bed. My money was hidden well, and my brother was still at home if I needed anything from there. I decided I could get by.

Moving to Chicago energized my marijuana game. It opened up the big city, free for the taking. It took some time to build relationships, but I put in the work and enjoyed great results. The next year, Timmy was graduating, and he called me in a panic.

"Jimmy, she kicked me out. I have nowhere to go. There's a box of your stuff and a box of mine, and that's it. Mom filed for bankruptcy and lost the house. They moved somewhere else, and I'm on my own."

I knew what he was feeling—the baby bird had been kicked out of the nest, and it was fly or die.

"Timmy, you can come and stay with me. We'll figure it out. What's up with the house?"

"I don't know. The bank gave us a few months, but Mom found a new place and left with the rest of the family. She told me to leave."

"Well, then, let's say goodbye to the house in the only way you and I can. Let's go out with a bang! I'll pick you up this weekend. Tell all your friends to be at the house Friday night or Saturday night. We're gonna party all weekend long!"

And did we ever! We had at least twenty kegs out there on Skyline and a couple of local bands, and everyone swam all weekend in our Skyline home pool. There were beautiful girls in bikinis—or naked—all over the property. It was a pool kegger party for the ages. There were hundreds of people at the house—people sleeping in the empty rooms, people passed out in the bathrooms, and people strewn across the yard. It was an amazing way to say goodbye to the house we loved. I'm sure the bank didn't appreciate the mess they found when they finally took possession. But they could never prove we had anything to do with it.

I loved that house and all the memories I had growing up there. It was always my intention to buy it back and keep it myself, but I never did. Now, I drive by once in a while, and even though it's changed hands a few times, the big barn is still in the back, and those two damn boulders that were on the sides of the bus stop at the top of the hill are still where Dad put them all those years ago.

CHAPTER 4

CHI-TOWN IS MY OYSTER

My life and my business grew in a big way when I moved deep into Chicago. My buddy Kevin, who'd been on the wrestling team with me, moved there too, and my little brother joined us now and then after he graduated before eventually staying full-time. All of us had been tight since we were kids—we had found the weed together and had made life-altering money together, and I never saw that changing. The only people I trusted in that business were my childhood friends. That trust was one of the things I felt made me successful.

One day when we were all together, Robbie brought up the idea of going to the Navy recruiting office to sign up. The Navy was the last thing on my mind. Being cooped up on a ship for months at a time without a decent meal or the warm body of a gorgeous hottie next to me was not my idea of a good time. But we all went downtown to check it out. We had each taken the ASVAB tests in high school on career day, so all they had to do was pull up our records. As each of my buddies went into the office with the recruiter to discuss aptitude and career options, I sat there patiently. I don't think I actually believed any of them would ever leave the life we had. When it was my turn to go in, I knocked and opened the door. The recruiter, Sergeant First Class McGuire, asked my name, and he typed it into his computer with a diligent two-finger peck.

"Listen, I'm just here to support my friends. I don't think I want to join the Navy. No offense."

"Oh—here we are, James Keene. Well, based on your testing, you pretty much qualify to do any kind of job in the Navy you want. That's pretty impressive! We could use more guys like you in the service."

"Nah, I'm good, honestly. I'm going to play football. Just—if any of the guys ask, tell them I did it. Okay?" I walked out smiling and shaking his hand.

The truth is, I had always thought I'd go pro in football, or I would become a cop. The latter idea never made my father happy. Kankakee was not the kind of environment where children dreamed of becoming doctors or lawyers, or ballerinas. All such dreams were efficiently crushed as kids watched their parents work half to death to make so little that they could barely support their families. The only dream that anyone held onto was getting the fuck out of that city. And the only means of escape available to us kids was excelling at sports. If you were extremely smart, got a full-ride scholarship, and had everything paid for, maybe you could work through it until you were employable with a good salary. But most kids followed in their parents' footsteps, working in the factories, being police officers, or working in the lounges, casinos, etc.

I remember visiting my dad one day when I was still in high school after we had been talking about me becoming a cop over the previous months. When I arrived, he had several of his police officer friends at the house, all upper-ranking officers with their full brass on. I thought they were going to encourage me to join the force. I was so excited to talk to them about their wild adventures and saving lives. But that wasn't the conversation we had. They told me about the high likelihood of being shot in the face due to the high crime rate we had in the city. They told me about the meager compensation they received for putting their lives on the line and about every negative thing you could imagine about being a police officer. They said I was too talented, and that I was too good to stay in lowly, industrial Kankakee in a dead-end civil career. I was better off following my dad's advice, playing sports, and going pro. They put extreme pressure on me not to become a police officer and to go do something better. I felt confused by all of it.

There wasn't much my hometown could offer its young people. At one time, Kankakee was actually voted the worse place to live in the United States, with the highest crime rate in the nation and the highest unemployment rate in the state. But when you grow up in a place like that, you become numb to the violence and poverty all around you, and when you see things happen that would leave someone else with night terrors for life, you barely even flinch. You just move on.

Within the next couple of months, Both Robbie and Kevin had joined the Navy and were shipping out. A few other friends that were with us at the recruitment office that day did as well. My crew was dwindling fast. Without a crew that I could trust, I knew I might end up at the bottom of the lake if I wasn't careful. That's when my lifelong friend Pauly became my right-hand man. He was a double economics graduate from Illinois University, he handled all my business's books and records, and I grew to trust him more than almost anyone. Still, due to my entrepreneurial ways and memories of poverty, I watched over him and my books and records like a hawk.

Pauly was also on the regional board of one of the largest health club chains in the country. This allowed us twenty-four-hour access to the largest health clubs in the city and Chicagoland area. Because of Pauly's high-ranking position in the company, we were able to use the private executive locker rooms, where you had to have a special key to get in. Pauly also oversaw all the members allowed in those locker rooms, so this offered us the unique opportunity to use any of more than fifty health clubs in the Chicagoland area to stash and store large loads of money and product. One locker could hold a substantial amount of product or millions of dollars in cash. Pauly and I were the only ones who had a key to all the Chicagoland executive health clubs, so we had total control of those areas. It also enabled us to stay mobile. Moving from one executive health club location to the next made it almost impossible for law enforcement to pinpoint our exact locations or get search warrants for a whole chain of company locations. It was a very unique addition to our overall operation.

Next, I added Big Bryan and Big Reg. Both were muscular giants from my football and wrestling teams and were lifelong friends. Big Bryan was White and Big Reg was Black, and both were extremely intimidating, towering pillars of fear with some serious presence no one could ignore. Both had grown up with me and knew my martial arts and wrestling skillsets were superior to theirs—not to mention my hard-to-match street fighting skills—so if I barked, they listened. However, their size and presence completed my crew's powerful strength. Both were extremely loyal to me.

Finally, I added Johnny O. to the crew, who was also a reliable lifelong friend from wrestling and martial arts. Since high school, Johnny had become a talented lawyer, and he soon became my personal consigliere.

Around age twenty, I was inducted into the Chicago mafia due to my heritage, reputation, and due to having friends who were high up in the organization. I think the mob felt less threatened by having me in their ranks, but I still did my own thing as well. We would sell to each other if either of us was short on product.

At one point, there was major political uproar in the Gulf, and product from Panama was not making it through the Florida Gulf ports into the United States. That area was the main source of the mafia's product at the time, so I wasn't surprised when I was called at home by one of the main capos about my ability to procure product through other avenues.

"Jimmy, the boss needs product, and he feels it's time for you to pay tribute—if you're one of us, you need to give us part of the deal—same price, straight across."

Being the businessman that I am, I did not find this acceptable. I considered my words with care. "You know I respect the Don. We have a good thing going, he and I, and of course I want to help. But it's not fair for me and my crew. We put a lot on the line to obtain those goods and bring them in without being detected, so we have to keep something in return."

He laughed. "See, the Don considers *you* as part of his crew—his family. Why would you take a part of his cut like that? You want the family to suffer? Would you do that to your brothers?"

"I mean no disrespect to Don, but is he planning to share his men and resources to help me get that product past the Feds? I've gotta support my men and my operation, and there's no way around it. I can supply the Boss and your crew, but only after he pays us a fair price."

"That's not going to fly, Jimmy. Go have a sitdown with the boss tonight and tell him that yourself, or you'll be in hot water. He'll be very disappointed if you don't show," he said.

It was important to my survival to maintain friendly ties with the Chicago mob, so I did as he demanded, hoping the Don would see things my way and decide that he needed my supply more than I needed a shakedown. I didn't have any plans to change my decision. I also knew that I had to hold my ground, or they would likely pull me into their whole empire until my entire enterprise and all of its profits were under their control.

As I sat across from the boss of all bosses that evening in his opulent study, he smiled at me magnanimously as though I were his favorite son. "Jimmy you are like a son to me and I have great respect for you and all you have accomplished, and right now you're the man with the connections that we need to remove us from this dry spell. We need product, and you're the one who can provide it. It's time to prove your loyalty—to uphold your oath. You'll be richly rewarded, but first you must make this deal. How can you ask more of your family than what you paid? We're expecting great things from you, Jimmy." He leaned forward as if to draw me into his confidence and clasped his fingers in front of him, his heavy gold rings glinting in the light. "If you let me down, Keene, I'll be very displeased."

I met his gaze firmly but respectfully. "Boss, if you need supply, I can get it for you. But I can't budge on the price. My crew has expenses and expectations, and you can't imagine all I've gone through to acquire these connections and get these prices. Surely as the leader of such a great organization yourself, you know that I can't give you what you're asking. I won't change my mind. Let me know when you're ready to proceed, and I'll have your product right away at the best price anywhere. Of course, I mean no disrespect. I value our relationship."

His gaze was impassive, but his eyes lit with a predatory spark that I was not unfamiliar with. "As much as I like you be careful, Jimmy. You'll be hearing from us." He waved his hand to dismiss me, and I left, the threatening ambiguity behind his last statement shooting an involuntary jolt up my spine.

In a matter of days, I heard whispered rumors through my contacts that the Don had put out a hit on me and wanted me gone. One night as I walked to my car, I felt eyes watching me from the shadows of the street, and I knew they were waiting for the right time to strike. I knew how this worked. If I wouldn't meet their demands, they would make an example of me instead and beat my crew into submission until they answered only to the mob. But I was ready and waiting, too. I knew they were desperate for product, and I was their last option. If they took me out it wouldn't be easy, and it'd take a lot of resources for them to recreate the services I could provide. It was a gamble, but it was an important one, and I had one hell of a poker face.

By the time another week had passed, his capo called again. "Listen, Jimmy. The boss has decided to be merciful to you. He will accept your deal *this* time. Get us the product—now."

The Don had realized a slightly higher price was better than no product at all. I wasn't worth as much to them dead, even if they did have to pay a higher price for what I had to offer. With my goods coming directly through Mexico, I was basically the only heavy hitter getting any product in at all, and they had to meet my terms. The game was over, and I had won.

I knew it was important to set up legitimate businesses for cleaning money, but buried deep down, I dreamed of making a certain amount of money, getting out of the game, and going legit for good. Always watching your back, staying a step ahead of law enforcement, and keeping drug dealers on good terms was an exhausting business. We encountered landmines all around us, from crooked police task forces to murderous, crazy street-thug gangbangers. There was always danger around the next corner. But as dangerous and difficult as it was, the lifestyle was intoxicating and highly addictive—especially for someone like me who grew up in poverty and always dreamed of the sort of life I'd achieved. But it was lonely.

When it came to women, I never knew if they were with me because of who I was or just for my money and to be with the sort of wild-eyed bad boy I was known to be. There are some bad girls out there. I was always smart enough to know when I was dealing with a bad chick. I'd just have fun with them for a night or two and then be gone. That would really fuck with them. Some of those girls were so alluring you could feel your eyebrows curl from the heat of their presence—seductively sublime women whose physical beauty couldn't be matched. But a beautiful face doesn't make a beautiful person inside. I learned that early in life.

Even though I was sexually attracted to a girl and wanted to have sex with her, I knew I didn't need that type of freight train to run me over on the tracks and turn my life into a chaotic nightmare. For my own self-preservation, I would always split early on. When girls would come around who I could see were genuine and could be trusted, I treated them like queens. That's what really meant something to me. I've had my share of stunningly beautiful women since I was young, but a genuine woman who understood my lifestyle—full of wild parties, strippers, and entertaining dangerous guests—but still truly loved me, was a woman who had my respect.

CHAPTER 5

THE HEAT IS ON

The business was booming and moving into neighboring states. Our friend Jose from South Chicago just couldn't produce as much product as I felt we needed and would be able to move in my rapidly expanding network. I decided it was time to find a cartel connection to use primarily and still have access to Jose and his weed as needed. But it's not like you can pick up the yellow pages and have an assortment of cartel phone numbers at your disposal. I had to find someone who could vouch for me and who was already dealing with a cartel so I could win my way in. Vouching is a serious commitment. Your ass is on the line, and if anything goes south, you might end up in a barrel in the desert.

Looking back, there were better places to store weed than a deserted ranch warehouse in the middle of the desert. But we were kids. Our assets were few, so we worked with what we had. Out west, we had a ranch and Richie O'Reilly.

Richie probably smoked half of what we brought in, but he was our buffer. Tim and I handled the financials, but Richie knew the market. He knew people in and out of the cartels. Between shipments, he stored the goods under a shitty warehouse on a shitty ranch in the middle of the shitty Arizona desert. He seemed to live close enough that I wondered if he wasn't just living there full-time. If he did, he didn't clean up much. The place was a wreck on a good day. And in the dry spell? Christ, no thanks.

The dry spell came and went with summer, and for three months every year, buying weed was damn near impossible. Dealers may as well have smoked cash, the way it ruined the trade. But if you made it work, autumn might find you as king of the mountaintop.

The worst dry spell I ever experienced was in the early '80s. Spring ended early that year, and the heat followed. Even the cartels got nervous. Nothing would grow—weed, coca, nothing. The notion of thriving left our priority list. That summer, all Tim and I did was survive. What else could we do—pray? No, I could only hope that something would come my way.

So, when Richie left a voicemail for me early one morning in July and told me to call him, saying that he knew a guy that could get things flowing again, I saw that I'd hoped enough. I saw my ticket to the mountaintop. I called him immediately.

The phone rang for less than a second before he picked up. I could hear him breathing through the phone like he'd been jogging in place next to it.

"Hey, Jimmy. Listen, Jimmy. I've got this friend out here. His name's Jeff. He's the real deal. Says he can get us as much as we need. A thousand pounds, two thousand pounds—whatever. But he wants to meet you, and he wants you to fly out here."

Richie paused to take a breath. I waited a moment for him to catch up.

"Great, Richie. Anything else?"

"No, that's it." He swallowed. "I think it's a good deal. What do you think?"

I opened the kitchen window and stuck my arm out. Minutes ago, as my girlfriend April and I walked home, the early Chicago air had been pleasant if a bit humid. Now it was starting to burn. I hadn't been out to Phoenix in months, but I figured it couldn't be worse. Even if it were, I would be back tonight or tomorrow morning.

I withdrew my hand and shut the window. "I can meet him today."

Five hours later, I waved Richie down outside Sky Harbor's brand-new Terminal 3. He waved back, his dark brown hair flapping in the wind, before pulling his head back into the passenger window of Jeff's ride. The grey Chevy station wagon was in peak condition, not a scratch to be found. I noticed it didn't have a front license plate. Odd.

As the driver pulled up to the curb a few yards to my right, a pit formed in my stomach. No backplate either.

"Door's open," Richie said from the passenger seat. He waved his hand toward me, then the driver. "Jimmy, Jeff. Jeff, Jimmy."

I opened the right-side door and stepped in to greet our guy. As Jeff turned back toward me, the pit in my stomach shriveled, and whatever I'd planned to say died in my throat.

Jeff's dark brown hair was even longer than Richie's but was trapped under a featureless, black baseball cap. His old sunglasses, the lenses filthy, rested on a nose that'd been broken and poorly set in excess. If this guy was a cop—and he most certainly was—he was terrible at pretending not to be.

"Hey," he said.

"Hey," I said. *How to play this?* "I hear you can help us out."

Jeff turned and put the station wagon—no plates— in drive. "Yeah. Me and my guys, we can get all the weed you need. I hear you got a place to keep it out here?"

I looked at Richie. "Tell me about your guys."

Jeff snorted. "Tell you—my guys? The fuck do you care, man?"

I shrugged. No one saw. "I like to know who's moving my product."

Richie looked at me like I'd just eaten cardboard. Jeff shook his head and laughed like a vulture.

"All right, man. Me and my guys—your Chi-Town ass would call us a biker gang. They have their own lines, but they all answer to me. One of them knows a guy who knows a guy, and I met the guy, and he's been growing for decades. So much that he's come out on top of every dry spell he's ever worked in."

The station wagon, no plates, lurched to a stop as a slow Ford truck with a bounty of hay in the back bed pulled out in front of us, hay showering the windshield. Jeff slammed his fist on the horn, but the only sound I heard was Jeff's frustrated expletive. His face turned red in the rearview mirror. He took his foot off the brake and eased forward.

"Anyway, the guy just cut ties with his biggest buyer, and we got him. Now, we got you. A thousand pounds, five thousand pounds, a few ounces, whatever—if you're in, my guys will get it, show it, and ship it. That enough for you?" Jeff leaned back against the headrest. "Or did you want their fucking names, too?"

I looked at Richie. A crooked, brown strand of hair lay against his seat. I plucked and threw it to the seat beside me only to find another one on my shirt. One thing I can say about Richie is that he had great hair; he was the spitting image of Rick Springfield when he was in his prime. Once again, Richie had proven to be the expert.

I leaned forward. "Yeah, that's enough. Let's talk price.

When I returned to Chicago later that night, I felt good. For three days, I felt good—excited even! And three days later, when the high had faded, when Jeff's grey station wagon—no plates (why couldn't I stop fixating on the damn plates?)—pulled up to the curb of Terminal 3, I felt the same pit forming in my gut. I had broken bread with this guy, but he was still wearing old sunglasses, his hair was still trapped under a black baseball cap, and he still looked like a cop—a cop that sucked at his job, but still a cop. The only difference between this and our first meeting was that Richie wasn't here with us, and I had a gym bag with two million dollars inside.

Jeff rolled down the window as I approached the vehicle.

"You got the money, right?" he asked, louder than I would have liked.

"Yeah, but let's see the product first." I opened the car door and hovered outside. "Cool?"

Jeff pressed back into his seat, unbothered. "Cool. Hop in."

This is not cool. This is a damn setup. But I'd come this far, and Jeff talked a big game. Besides that, Richie hadn't failed us yet. Not in a big way, at least. So, I sat in the passenger seat, shut the door, and rolled up the window. Jeff peeled the car away from the curb and set out.

We didn't speak. There was rarely a need to when it came to this sort of thing. It wasn't like riding with family—silence wasn't uncomfortable, it was welcome.

I looked around the car. I hadn't noticed last time, but like the exterior, the interior was impeccable. I half expected to find a 9mm pistol and a tin can of cigarette butts stashed behind my seat. No such thing. The leather seats smelled like they'd just been cleaned. Jeff said he was a biker, but what kind of biker drove a clean car?

Ten minutes later, having driven across town, I found Jeff was telling the truth, or at least part of it. As he pulled into the parking lot of the Starbird Inn, I saw five men around back, three of whom had the same featureless, black baseball caps as Jeff. Each one sat on a motorcycle parked right outside the hotel doors. Three more bikes were parked nearby. Inside the window next to the hotel doors, I saw their owners, two with hats, pretending not to notice our arrival. All of them were White, all of them were big and buff, and none of them was subtle.

Jeff looked at me and nodded. "Weed's in room thirteen."

I coughed, more out of shock than anything else. "Jeff, what's this?"

"What's what?"

I waved one hand toward the hotel doors. Jeff followed the motion, and his gaze rested upon the gang a little too long for my liking.

"Oh, them. These are my partners. 'My guys,' you know? The gang."

"The gang. Fuck." I opened the car door and stepped out, careful not to loosen my grip on the gym bag. "You honestly think I'm going to walk inside that hole with what I'm carrying?"

I leaned against the open door, ready to humor Jeff when he followed, which he didn't. He spoke through the doorway.

"What, man? What's the issue? Room thirteen."

I lowered my head to look at him. "Look, Jeff. I may be eighteen, but I'm not an idiot. And I'd wager that you either think I'm an idiot, or you're terrible at this."

"What do you want from me, man?"

"I want you to humor me. I'm going to go get a room. Somewhere else. You call me when you've got the goods somewhere neutral—where I won't get shot in the head."

Jeff bristled. He looked out at his crew. In retrospect, the look on his face should have confirmed everything. I knew it, Jeff knew it, the guys at the hotel knew it—this was a scam. A setup. I may as well have burned the money myself. But I was still riding that high. I was still trying to climb that mountain. I still had two million pressed against my back. My seed money. The only big money I had to my name. I wouldn't quit without a fight. I had to see this through.

Jeff tapped the steering wheel of the station wagon, no plates. "Sure, man. I didn't think. This is where we hang, but it makes sense on your end. Let me think."

He thought. So did I. Maybe he was terrible at this, but if nothing else, I hadn't heard gunshots. So, I waited.

"All right. Give me two hours. I'll move the stuff to a neutral spot. You bring the money; I'll have everything ready. Just you and me. None of my guys. They're waiting to move another shipment anyway."

I slapped the edge of the doorframe twice before walking off. "That's better. I won't go far. Call when you're ready."

And two hours later, he called. I hadn't left my room. By 11 a.m., it was too hot for anything else. I only wondered for a moment how he found me, but there weren't many hotels on this side of town. He'd probably called more than one asking for "that young Chi-Town ass." Our conversation was short.

"Jimmy?"

"That's me."

"Stuff's ready in a special spot out in the desert. My guys moved it and bailed. No one's even watching it. You ready?"

"You bet."

"Good. See you soon, man."

Five minutes later, there he was out front of the Marriott. Still in the grey station wagon, no plates. Between the hat, the glasses, and the shattered nose, I barely knew what this guy looked like. Terrible presentation, really. But even if he was terrible at this, maybe he'd picked things up more recently than I had. Maybe he was looking for an opportunity like I was. Maybe he just needed someone to teach him the ropes.

It sure as hell wouldn't be me. I got in the car anyway.

We drove. We drove far, far into the desert—so far that in an instant we were driving up the side of a mountain, and the pavement turned to dirt, and the dirt started to look out of place. If I died out here no one would know for decades. Perfectly neutral.

As the road curved and turned around the mountainside, Jeff turned to me. For the entirety of the curve, he kept his eyes off the road. For the first time, I thought this guy wasn't a cop. A cop wouldn't drive like an idiot on a mountain ridge.

"All right, man. As soon as we come around this bend here, you're going to see a whole bunch of cactuses. You're going to see a whole bunch of boxes, like refrigerator boxes, hidden in the group of cactuses. The weed's in those boxes."

The station wagon, no plates, lurched over a pothole. Jeff didn't seem to notice.

"And that's it. I'll stay in the car. You can go and check it out. Check one box, every box, I don't care. But it's all there. You look at it. If you like how it looks, I'll drive you back to town, you'll give me the money, and it's all yours to do what you want with. Cool?"

I looked at Jeff. I looked at the inside of the station wagon, no plates. I looked out at the open road and the dirt that curved ahead of us like alien pavement in a world I didn't recognize. I looked out at the red mountains to the north. They were short and wide—hardly what I'd call mountaintops. But they'd do. Tim and I had started small. We'd climbed higher in the last few years but taking it slow was getting old. I hated looking up. It was time to climb.

"Cool. Let's see it."

"All right." Jeff looked back at the road. As if on cue, the bend straightened out, and there they were a bunch of "cactuses," most ten feet or taller, distributed among what might later become a lookout point or a parking lot or a graveyard. Between them were a couple dozen crates. The kind they'd ship a refrigerator in.

Jeff pointed toward them as if there was anything else to look at. "There it is."

Despite everything, I felt better. "There it is. Can't wait."

The station wagon, no plates, pulled to a stop about twenty yards away from the setup. Without a word, I opened the car door and walked out, gym bag still slung over my shoulder. I didn't turn to see Jeff's reaction. Instead, I kept walking.

If this was legitimate, Tim and I were set. Our two million, our seed money, our livelihood made green, would change hands. We'd get what was probably the only weed in a two-thousand-mile radius. We'd sell it to someone—anyone, really. Anyone who could afford it could afford to double, triple, or quadruple what we'd paid for it. And with four million, eight million, sixteen million, we could keep growing and climbing higher and higher, and finally, we'd reach the damn mountaintop and someday get out of the business altogether. We—no, I deserved it.

I approached the nearest crate. Pure instinct said it was a trap, that it would blow up in my face. I kicked it. The box toppled over empty.

I wanted to shut my eyes and hang my head. Instead, I looked out over the edge of the future lookout point or parking lot or very soon-to-be graveyard. Other short, red mountaintops looked back. Stumpy, aspiring lumps among flat sand. Mountains in Arizona were pathetic.

Fuck. I turned around.

Ten yards away, halfway between me and the car, stood Jeff. I knew that the 9mm he pointed at my head was real, that my gut instinct had been right, that it would be very easy to shoot me and take everything I'd worked for right out of my hands, but it didn't scare me. No, Jeff had taken off his sunglasses. That scared me.

"Give me that money, motherfucker, or you're dead. Give me that fucking money!"

On instinct—I'd be listening to that from now on—I took a step back. "Hey, look. Jeff, man. What is this? I thought this was a straight deal here."

Jeff took two steps forward. He spat on the dirt as if to prove he was everything he claimed to be. Honestly, I believed it. "Shut up, motherfucker. Give me that money, or you're dead!"

For every step I took back, Jeff took two. It wouldn't be long before I fell into a few cactuses or tripped on a box or just fell off the side of the ridge, and then he'd be right. Dead. I started thinking for once. My thoughts were patchy, condensed, but they were there.

Okay. 9mm. Pistol, short barrel. Ideally, ten, fifteen-yard range. Bullet'll break down and bend. More slope, more speed, more angle to throw off the accuracy. We break and run.

"Give me that money, motherfucker, or you're dead! Give me that fucking money!"

Looking back, I wondered if he'd practiced that line in the mirror. "Jeff, I can't believe this, man. I thought this was a legitimate deal, man."

I turned on my ankle and booked it. Immediately, I heard pops, and dirt flew at my feet. I heard the box I'd kicked explode like a paper bomb. Three shots in an instant. But by then I was past the cactuses—*cacti, damnit*—and running down the slope of the mountain. Now I was out of range, at least the ideal. If he knew that, he didn't show it. Three more shots, four, five, all at my feet. All missed, some behind and straight, others ahead and curved.

"Fuck! I knew this was a setup. Fucking Richie!" The desert answered with a gust of wind that blew dust up into my face.

I was still alive and still running. Forty, fifty, a hundred yards out, I was still carrying two million, and Jeff was still sliding down the mountain, and bullets were still flying, and I could still run a four-three forty-yard dash, and despite everything, my dad would still be proud that I could run that fast, and Jeff was the shittiest drug lord I'd ever met, but he still had a gun and I was still just out here in the desert running for my life.

At the base of the mountain a hundred yards out, I saw a white break wall, the kind that carries water and gives life this far out. A godsend. I vaulted over the three-foot structure and felt something graze my wrist as I kept running. I looked down and saw the trickle of hot blood. The bullet had barely touched me, but the mark it left burned. It was not enough to make me panic, but I knew I had to move faster. I turned back and saw Jeff hauling ass up the ridge. Dumbass had followed me halfway down before he'd started thinking.

Straight ahead, miles beyond the break wall, was another mountain. Suddenly I didn't think Arizona peaks were so bad. However, many yards out, I looked over my shoulder again. I saw the grey station wagon, plates be damned, haul ass up the side of the ridge. Jeff was looking for a better angle. It wouldn't be hard to find. I kept running, but there was nothing—sand and rock and not much else. A few mountains here and there. And even if it was still morning, it was getting close to noon, and I could still remember the big, red "115" on the weather report I'd seen earlier today.

I concluded that one did not have to be stupid to die in the desert.

A quarter of a mile out, at the base of the nearest peak, inches before I started the upward ascent, I felt dirt kick up near my feet. I looked up at the towering stub I had blindly approached and saw Jeff with his sunglasses and that stupid hat. No, not Jeff. Jeff had the car. This guy had a bike. This guy had a revolver.

I turned on my heel again, this time out into the empty landscape toward the next mountaintop. Between me and the distant safety—if it was that—a pile of rocks erupted from the earth. Rocks and boulders—what beautiful, beautiful tools for someone dodging gunfire. I dove between them and immediately felt relief. My new cover was tall enough to shield me from bullets, but it would also shield me from the blinding sun, at least for a few minutes.

I tried to laugh. Instead, sand clogged my windpipe, and I coughed. "Richie, I swear to God, if I see you again, I'll beat your skull in."

The gym bag lay at my feet, still intact, no holes. I was alone in the desert and was probably going to die of thirst before Jeff and his cronies filled my corpse with lead just to prove a point, but I still had two million in cash, so it could have been worse.

I sat for a few minutes. There wasn't much I could do but catch my breath. They knew I wasn't armed, and they knew I had a bag with more money than they'd ever seen or would see again. I knew they wouldn't drive out into the sand—for once, I was glad to be dealing with bikers—and I knew, or at least hoped, that they wouldn't follow on foot. This was home to them. They knew how easy it was to die out here. All they had to do was wait.

"Fuck that." I stood up and peered over the edge of the boulder. I'd caught my breath again. In the distance, less than a mile north, I saw the grey station wagon, no plates, sitting on the ridge of Jeff's mountaintop. No Jeff in sight. Closer to me, to the west, I saw the other Jeff standing in front of his bike. He knew that I knew he saw me, because a patch of sand exploded near the boulder. I didn't move. He couldn't hit me this far away, not with a revolver. But he could wait.

Wait. I scanned the area and looked around the boulders I'd claimed. All around me, like a lopsided egg, I saw eight red, stubby mountaintops. In that moment, I would have bet two million that every single one of them had a Jeff with a bike on it, waiting for me to crawl up the side so he could shoot me in the head.

"Okay. Cool. Cool, cool cool, Richie. Good move. Good guy. Good deal. Good God, you fucking idiot." I turned and slid down the side of the boulder. The shade had vanished—in just a few minutes, the sun had risen to its height. Meltdown at high noon.

I looked out to the east—the only direction that really had nothing. Like the tip of the egg, the mountaintops rounded out and ended some ten, fifteen miles out. If I could make it past the edge, into the nothing, I might be able to find... Christ, anything but this. I could only see so far. I knew I might—no, I knew I probably would die, but at least I could bury this damn money in a sandpit. Maybe Tim would find it somehow. If nothing else, it'd make for one last "fuck you" to Jeff.

"Cop, my ass." I stood and slung the bag over my shoulder. I took a breath and tried to swallow the last of my spit. It stuck to my throat like sap.

Just like the mighty Achilles didn't let a stone steal his glory during his battle with Hector, I wasn't going to let the desert or Jeff steal my glory or end my life and my relentless climb to the top of the mountain. I would rather have heard my dad say it, but my own voice would have to do. "Run, son."

I booked it. I ran. Dry spell, be damned. I ran more than I would ever run again. The whole time, with every peak I passed, I heard the cracks and pops of gunfire and the dull thuds of bullets in sand. None of them hit me. Only a few came close, but with so many bullets, I knew I was right. There were more than two Jeffs here, and every one of them had a gun. I felt like an unwilling participant in a real-life video game. I was the target, and the two million dollars was the prize.

I stopped telling myself they wouldn't come down, but not because I didn't think it was true—because I couldn't think. I was bone dry. My saliva turned to sand, and my blood to dust. Gone. Empty. I couldn't feel the jagged air that cut my lungs. I couldn't get excited when I spotted the strip mall.

I'd never seen a mirage, obviously. Chicago was a reasonable city with water and air conditioning. But I knew a mirage when I saw one because I'd seen movies. I wasn't falling for it. I hadn't even run the full ten or fifteen miles. It wasn't even one in the afternoon. I'd give up in a few hours and let the vultures take me later.

"Fuck off, mall!" I roared and pawed at the air as if to drive the image away. But it remained. It shimmered in the heat, plowed through my parched psyche, and rooted itself there. It wouldn't leave, no matter how I screamed. I shouldn't have, but I screamed. Often.

I realized I couldn't scare the mirage away. I stopped running. For the first time since I'd left the plane, I dropped the bag. I slapped my face, rubbed my eyes, and then rubbed out the sand I'd just put in my eyes. I looked out east beyond what I'd seen from the safety of my boulders.

The strip mall was still there. It was real.

"God, it's real. It's a little fucking town." I lingered on the sight a little too long and felt sand strike the back of my leg. I leaped and twisted into the air and looked to the south. The nearest mountaintop, flatter and lower than the rest—*Fuck this state, these aren't mountains*—stood a few hundred yards away. I could see another Jeff standing by a motorcycle. He was probably as surprised as I was when the bullet almost hit me. I heard more shots. Without missing a beat, I grabbed the bag and ran. Again.

I made the last hundred yards to the strip mall in a limping sprint, but I made it. My ankle buckled when it stepped onto pavement, more out of joy than anything else. Structure. Sweet, sweet, stone structure. My ancient Stone Age ancestors had proven correct. Stone was the way of the future.

I stood on wobbly feet and looked around, trying to find the best thing to lie down and die next to. *No! Not today.* I looked around to find the best place to think of a plan instead. Of the eight or so stores I saw, the only one I recognized was Sam's Club. I'd been to

Sam's Club. Sam could be trusted. I lumbered across the parking lot to the entrance.

The security guard caught me before I fell against the front doors. I couldn't hear what he was saying. I croaked and slid against his grip, and before I knew it, I was leaning against the front wall, and he was pouring water down my throat. I choked and sputtered, nearly vomiting the joy right up. But I sucked the water down, and immediately, I knew that I would live—at least long enough to die by gunshot like a man.

"Hey, hey. Take it easy. You okay? What the hell happened?" The security guard—*what the hell is this kid in an apron doing guarding a store?*—held his hands up, unsure if he should help me up or start throwing punches.

"Yeah, man, I'm okay." I slung the gym bag over my shoulder. "You got a phone around here?"

The security guard had to be twenty-one to have that pistol, but with the freckles peppering his face he looked no older than sixteen. He looked at me like I'd asked him to kill the president. He thumbed over his shoulder. "Payphone is around the corner by the newspaper stand."

"Great. Thanks for the drink." I clapped him on the shoulder and moved behind him. After confirming that there was a payphone uncomfortably close to the newspaper stand and that it would take the phone card

I kept for this horrible, horrible state, I turned back to the kid. He hadn't moved.

"Hey, you. Get inside and call the police."

"What?"

"Some biker gang's coming to town to stir up trouble. Get the police here, tell them there are eight or so guys with 9mm pistols, shots have been fired, and they've already hit one man."

The guard stood there a moment as if to weigh his options. I was about to yell at him to get to it when he opened the front doors and ran inside.

I turned back to the payphone and leaned on the newspaper stand. I pulled out the phone card and dialed Tim's number.

"This is Tim."

"Tim, thank God. Listen—Jeff, the goods—it's all a setup. I need you and the guys to come out here and take care of these guys. Get me the fuck out. Fuckin' Richie, that asshole! It's bad, Tim. It's a bad situation, they've—"

"Hell, Jimmy! Calm down. Take a breath."

I took a breath. It hurt.

Tim took a breath, too. It hurt to hear, as if my little brother were annoyed that I was calling at all. "Start over. What the fuck's going on?"

It took a few tries, but eventually, I got the whole story out. Jeff calling me, me flying out to meet him, the feeling in my gut, the hotel, the gang, the cactuses, the boxes, the gun, more guns, the desert—all of it, probably too fast for Tim to absorb.

"Jimmy. Get the hell out of there. Get the money and get back to Chicago!"

"Yeah man, yeah, I am. I got to—" I stopped. There was a hole in the back of the newspaper stand. A raccoon, a coyote, or some other desert mongrel must have been starving because something had chewed a two-by-two-foot hole right through the wood. On a whim, I jammed the gym bag into the hole, forcing it upward so it couldn't be seen unless someone bought a newspaper. Judging by the date on the issue, I figured it'd be a day or two before that happened.

"Jimmy? Hello? Jimmy!"

"Yeah! Fuck, sorry man. I'm just—I just hid the money, but I'll remember where it is. They won't find it unless they buy a newspaper."

"Fucking what—?"

I stopped listening. I almost dropped the phone. A grey station wagon, no plates, pulled into the opposite edge of the parking lot.

"Jimmy! Man, answer me, you fucking—"

"I need to go, Tim. They're here. If I'm alive, I'll call you later." I hung up the phone.

The station wagon drove slowly around the perimeter of the strip mall, pausing around the entrance to each store. As it passed the first store, the roar of bikes echoed across the lot, and the gang poured in.

They drove faster than Jeff, riding in circles around cars and the few patrons of this burgeoning ghost town, but that was just scare tactics. Jeff was looking for me. It wouldn't be long before he got here, and I didn't trust the newspaper stand to take one bullet, let alone dozens.

I turned and ran back toward the rear of Sam's Club. There I found, to my primal glee, an L-shaped pile of concrete rubble. It must have been a wall at one point, the way it was angled against those trash cans. Maybe they were building a new one. Maybe they wouldn't notice if I took some.

I picked up the most manageable chunk I could find, which was just a bit smaller than a basketball. I didn't have a plan for it, but rocks had already saved my life once today, and the pavement at my feet was as real as the hell I had just run ten or fifteen miles through. If I was going to die here, I would do it on my terms—after I caved Jeff's skull in.

With the chunk in my hands, I lumbered back over to the newspaper stand. Farther away, most of the bikers were still riding in circles, but a few had peeled off to harass shoppers on the western side. The grey station wagon with no damn plates had rounded the interior corner of the strip mall and was coming my way slowly, meticulously. I wondered if Jeff had been here before, knew where the payphone was, and knew where I'd hidden the money. In a moment of furious panic, I stepped out into the lot.

The car stopped. Through the windshield, I saw Jeff in his stupid hat and stupid glasses with his stupid nose I wanted to break myself. I heard the window roll down, but he didn't stick his head out.

I raised the chunk of concrete to my chest. "Are you looking for me, motherfucker?"

Jeff floored it. In an instant, he was right there, and in an instant, I swung my arms back, launched the concrete, and dove for the newspaper stand.

I didn't see it, but I heard the glass shatter. I heard the shocks groan. I heard the tires screech. I heard steel grind against pavement. I heard a resonating crash, one that drowned out the roar of bike engines. I heard a gunshot, maybe a misfire. I heard the awe-struck silence of an American strip mall.

When I finally looked up, I saw the dusty, doorless wreckage of a bent and broken station wagon, no room for plates and more skid than grey. The wreckage lay pressed against the side of a yellow sedan, one of several cars it had crushed as it ground through the lot.

Looking back, I should have said something awesome, like "Don't fuck with my money," or "That's all it takes," or something about breaking Jeff's nose. Looking back, I think that would have made me feel better about the whole thing.

Instead, I limped over to the payphone. I called for a ride. I hid behind the newspaper stand as cops—real cops, the kind that drive cars with sirens and plates—yanked a bloodied, still-breathing Jeff from the wreckage. I watched them chase down and bag all the Jeffs on bikes.

When the taxicab drove up, I pulled the gym bag from the hole in the stand. I opened the door, looked once more at the most American strip mall I'd ever see, and told the driver to take me to Richie's place.

Looking back, I wish I'd kept the rock.

I wasn't going back to the hotel just in case the bikers had sent someone there to wait and see if I showed up. I had a bone to pick, and it wasn't gonna be fun. I went back to the warehouse and walked in. Richie was in the back with the small TV on, sitting on the couch and smoking some weed. When he saw me, his eyes started to dart back and forth, looking behind me and coming to the conclusion that there was nobody around me hauling in piles of weed. I could almost hear his mind turning and finally landing on the conclusion that I was pissed off.

"Fuck you, Richie! What the fuck was that about? 'I know this guy, Jimmy.'" I took a deliberate step in his direction. "'He's the real deal, Jimmy.'" Another step. "'HE CAN GET US AS MUCH AS WE WANT, JIMMY!!'" By this time, Richie was backing up urgently.

"Hey, man, what's wrong? I don't know what you're talking about."

"I've been out in the desert the entire day dodging bullets and running for my life!" I had Richie cornered against the wall, and if he could have scaled it like a lizard, he would have. I grabbed the collar of his shirt and twisted. Then I buried my fist in the wall right next to his head.

"You're a fucking idiot!" I pulled him off the wall, swung him around, and threw him on the floor. "I'm going to go wash my face, and you are taking me to the airport. If I stay another minute, I will fucking kill you!"

Richie knew if he didn't want his head smashed in, it was best to leave me alone to cool off. He knew he had fucked up. He had regret written all over his face as we drove back to Phoenix.

During my flight, I thought about growing up with Richie. I was torn. Man, I liked him. But this guy had become a complete fuck-up. I could have been killed thanks to Richie's incompetent, partying habits.

"I had a few drinks with him at the bar. We smoked a joint together." Richie's words burned in my brain. Richie had become a liability. He was the type of guy that liked to hang at the clubs chasing skirts around all the time. He wanted to see everything in life from a good-time-Charlie point of view, no matter what the situation was. Fuck! This whole deal had been fucked

up, and no matter how much I liked Richie, his haphazard behavior was bringing the heat on us.

Anticipating future events, I knew that Richie would draw unwanted attention to my organization and me. It would only be a matter of time before I'd have to tell Richie he was out.

When I arrived at O'Hare airport, I got my car and drove home. I pulled up to my house and trudged wearily up to the door and into the kitchen. April was busy making dinner. I pulled April close, savoring the feeling of her body against mine, grateful for the comfort she provided. Exhausted, I sat down at the table. She sat on my lap and kissed me.

"How was your day?"

I responded with a dry laugh. "You wouldn't believe me even if I told you."

She looked at me with those beautiful, sparkling eyes. Then, without a word, she wrapped her arms around me, holding me tight. I felt her soft lips against mine, and for a moment, all of my worries and stresses from the whole ordeal melted away.

I took her in my arms and pulled her close, feeling the warmth of her body against mine. She tilted her head back with a slight sigh, and I leaned down, brushing my lips against her neck.

They were soft, gentle kisses at first—a sweet reunion after a long day of travel. But as our lips met again, our kisses deepened, growing more urgent and passionate. I pulled her closer, feeling her hands slide up my back and her legs wrap around me as I sat on the kitchen chair. I could feel myself getting lost in the heat of the moment.

April pulled back, breathless, gazing into my eyes. I brushed a strand of hair from her face and leaned in for another kiss. I could feel my desire for her growing harder. All of the tension from my disastrous trip had built like water behind a dam inside me, and her touch felt like a hot stick of dynamite threatening to bust the barrier wide open and let all that pressure come rushing out. Feeling the warmth of her skin through her clothes, I started to explore more of her body with my hands. April let out a soft moan, overwhelmed by the intensity of me cradling her beautiful breasts through her tight T-shirt. I could tell she wanted me inside of her just as badly as I wanted to be there.

I stood up, April's legs still wrapped around me, our bodies pressed close together. The air between us was thick. I could feel her anticipation and desire for me to take control. I loved the way her eyes glimmered in the dim light as I slid her shirt off, unhooked her bra, and let all of it fall to my floor. Every touch seemed to send a shiver down her spine, and I could feel the heat radiating from her body as I caressed her bare skin.

April looked up at me, biting her lip nervously. She cupped my cheeks and pressed her lips against mine. It was a slow, tender kiss at first, like before, but again, her kisses became urgent and passionate.

With her mouth pressed to mine, she pleaded, "Jimmy, take me to bed I need to feel you inside me already!"

I sprinted to the bedroom with her wrapped tightly around my body, April giggling the whole way. April had a way of making my day end much better than it started. She always knew what I needed and delivered without me having to say a word.

CHAPTER 6

ONE NIGHT IN MEXICO

I learned a lot from my dad. I learned what really matters in life. More importantly, I learned how to protect what was mine. My dad's motto was, "Don't fuck with my family, and don't fuck with my community." That said everything that needed to be said about him. As for me, my motto was, "Don't fuck with me or my family, and don't fuck with my money." In that order—on most days. But the truth was, if you fucked with my money, you *did* fuck with my family because that would take away my means of caring for my family. Fucking with one fucked with the other. Anyone who knew anything about me understood this. I had a reputation for protecting what was mine, and I worked hard for that reputation. Because of the name I made for myself, I rarely had to worry about people trying to screw me over.

About six months after the shootout in the Arizona desert, we were still experiencing a serious dry spell.

My childhood friend Robbie had moved to Texas when he joined the Navy. As kids growing up, our whole crew of friends spent countless days at Kankakee River State Park rock and mountain climbing. The park was full of towering cliffs and mountainous rocks to climb, and we became adept at scaling them. Robbie knew that I was having trouble procuring a large quantity of weed and called to say he had a friend in Mexico, right on the border of Texas, who could supposedly get me all the weed we wanted. After my last attempt to procure product, I'd become more cautious, but we had to do something—our stash was drying up fast, and that meant no money coming in.

I swallowed any misgivings and immediately jumped on the opportunity. Tim and I gathered some of our crew and boarded a plane to Texas the next day. When we arrived, Robbie and a guy named Pat picked us up in a white van.

"We'll have to drive across the border to Mexico and pick up the goods," Robbie explained. "My guy wants to meet at a cantina down there."

"Fine," I agreed.

Robbie had kept up with rock and mountain climbing as a hobby even after he moved down to Texas. His gear clanked and dangled around us on the van's walls. The van was all beat up with no seats in the back, just a bunch of oversized beanbags tossed in that would slide around if you took a corner too fast. As we drove,

I played through several possible scenarios in my mind. I always tried to be three steps ahead of any situation, and today was no different. I zipped open my bag and fingered the cash inside. If what Robbie said was right, this would be the best five hundred thousand dollars I ever spent. There was no way I would take two million dollars into an unknown situation ever again. I'd brought enough cash to show them I was serious, and if things panned out the way they were supposed to, I had someone ready to fly out with the rest of the cash. After checking the satchel to ensure everything was in order, as was my habit, I zipped the bag closed and looped the strap over my shoulder.

We reached the rendezvous point two hours after landing, pulling the van behind the cantina that sat alone in an expanse of desolate land, made up only of the cantina and a parking area out front that connected to a dirt road. The road met up with the highway about three miles to the west. We went inside to wait.

The cantina was clean but still smelled of old whiskey spilled on the counters. The place looked like it would fall down if someone farted too hard, but I guess that was part of its Old-Mexico charm. We waited for a little while until a beat-up car pulled up and parked outside next to the van, and a heavily tattooed Mexican man with a mean scowl climbed out and made his way inside.

"Jimmy, this is Jorge." Robbie said, gesturing between us. I looked Jorge over and kept a close eye on him to see if he had a gun or not. He seemed fairly personable, despite the nasty expression on his face, but I'd never met him before, and I didn't trust easily.

I trusted my crew, but aside from that, trust was a hard thing to find in that line of work. Sure, there were a few business associates whom I trusted—at least, to some degree. I'm sure a few people trusted me—to the same degree. But even that form of trust was defined differently in my world than it was for most people. The general public throws that word, "trust," around like confetti at a parade. But in my world, that confetti was made of shrapnel that could shred you on impact. In the end, it was every man for himself, but there had to be a certain level of trust involved. The best way to define trust in my world was to call it an 'understanding.' That means, if you fuck with what's mine, you get fucked up, or you die. It was as simple as that.

"I don't have the goods with me," Jorge explained. "I have a stash house a little further south. You'll have to drive down there, but you can buy all the weed you need."

I instantly remembered Arizona. *Here we go again,* a little part of me thought, but I didn't want to miss this chance. Every hope I had rested on that dough. I was fearless to a fault and willing to take the risk. I was determined to get to the top of the mountain, and this was the only option I had at the moment to get there.

We drove deep into Mexico until we arrived in a scummy, run-down little village and pulled up behind Jorge in front of a little house. Jorge sauntered up to our van.

"Just Jimmy goes in with the money," he said coolly. I surveyed the scene. Despite the shady neighborhood, the house looked decent enough.

"Okay," I agreed. "I'll go in by myself." I followed Jorge up the short path and through the front door. As soon as the front door banged shut behind me, the hair stood up on the back of my neck. The house was empty—something was off. I followed Jorge to the kitchen where there was only a cheap and flimsy card table with a scale sitting on it set up in the middle of the room.

"Well, where's the weed?" I asked.

Jorge's eyes flicked around the room. He didn't look at me directly. "Oh no, no, no, don't worry. My guy's got it. He'll be here in a second."

Suddenly, five guys burst out of different back rooms, all pissed-off-looking Mexicans and all armed with machine guns that were pointing right at me.

Jorge's tone turned instantly frigid: "Give me the money, motherfucker, or you're dead!" The men shoved me against the wall and aimed their guns at my head.

"You fucker, Jorge. I couldn't move an inch. I breathed evenly to keep my wits sharp.

"Shut up man, or I'll have them kill you!" The men ripped my bag full of money out of my hands. "Now, keep your ass against that wall and count to one hundred. Move a muscle, and you're dead."

I had no choice. I did what Jorge said and counted until I heard them leave out the back door. Then I dashed out the front door and back to the van. I realized how lucky I was that they hadn't just shot me. Mexican drug runners don't think twice about killing anyone who gets in their way.

"Did you get it?" Tim asked.

I slammed my fist into the van's hood and then smashed in the door with an explosion of fury and electric adrenaline I couldn't contain. "It was a fucking setup. It was a rip-off!" I leaned into the van to yank Robbie out, banging up the dash in the process. "How in the fuck did you meet this Jorge and set this up?" I screamed at him, shaking his whole body with his shirt clenched in my hands.

Robbie frantically tried to shake himself free. "I'm sorry, dude," he choked out weakly. "I bought weed from him a few times, and he always seemed pretty straight."

I dropped him to the ground and turned around. "Yeah, well, when you got five hundred thousand dollars on the line, people get weird real fast."

It was obvious they were gone, and they'd taken off with all of my money.

I looked back at the house and realized it was just a dummy house. Nobody lived there. Drug runners used dummy houses to bring people in and convince them to get inside with their cash. Then the drug runners played them for all they were worth and robbed or in some cases killed them. I'd just fallen victim to a classic rip-off technique.

"Well, let's get out of here," Pat said. "It's starting to get dark, and we're gonna be stuck out here in Mexico."

I shook my head and turned to fix Robbie and Pat with a furious glare. "Oh no, no, no—we're not leaving here until I find this fucking guy and get my money back," I growled through a stiffened jaw. I didn't care that Jorge and his cronies had guns and we didn't. My blood boiled in my veins, and leaving wasn't an option. I felt unstoppable. There was no way in hell I was going home without my money. Jorge would be sorry that he fucked with me. *No one* sets me up, steals my fucking money, and gets away with it. He was going to learn that lesson firsthand.

I ordered everyone back into the van, and we drove up and down side streets in Mexico for two or three hours. Finally, I recognized a guy who was drunker than a skunk sniffing its own ass walking down the street. He was one of Jorge's machine-gun-toting side-kicks. This guy was easy pickings.

"There's one of Jorge's guys, right there," I shouted. We flew the van up right next to the guy, opened the sliding door, and my crewman Kevin grabbed the guy in a headlock, flipped him into the van, and shut the door. Kevin was a national wrestler with me in college, and he was my enforcer. Kevin wasn't as tough as me, but he was flat-out crazy and one of the toughest, badass street fighters I'd ever known. We tied Jorge's guy up and beat the shit out of him for an hour and a half until he told us where to find Jorge.

Jorge was in a local hotel that Jorge's guy claimed was impenetrable. We decided to look for ourselves. Even if we weren't gunning for him, the word 'impenetrable' would still have been too much of a temptation to pass up. Who wouldn't want the chance to take on that challenge? So, we headed straight for the hotel and looked through the front doors from a safe distance. If you could fit one more Mexican with a machine gun in that lobby, I would be surprised. If we just walked in there, they would make Swiss cheese of us in a hurry. We had to be smart.

We returned to the van to discuss our options. My crew was skeptical.

"Man, there's no way we can get in there," Robbie said, shaking his head.

Unwilling to give up, I paused to think and plan. I looked at all Robbie's rock-climbing gear on the van's wall and I said, "Oh, I'm going to find a way."

A few minutes later, Tim and I silently approached the fire escape on the backside of the building and climbed quickly to the top of the hotel. Who knew that all those careless summers spent rappelling off cliffs would come in handy one day against drug runners in Mexico? There was a swimming pool on the top of the building, but luckily no one was using it. As we went, we took notice of every guard we saw through the windows and quickly figured out that Jorge was on the ninth floor in a guarded room. Jorge also had armed guards on his whole hotel floor.

Once we'd gathered the intel we needed, we sprinted to the van (where Jorge's man was still gagged and tied) and grabbed two sets of climbing gear. We hurried back up the fire escape to the roof and prepared to rappel from the roof to Jorge's ninth-floor balcony.

The only weapon I had was a blackjack. As we scaled down the building and made our way to the balcony, I cursed myself for not carrying any guns with us on this trip. Why the hell would I do business with these thugs who could shoot me in the face at any given minute carrying nothing but a blackjack? *Well, it's gonna have to do; there's no turning back now.* We climbed over the patio railing and tried the patio door. It was unlocked. Of course it was! Who the fuck would enter a ninth-floor hotel room from the fucking balcony?

As we snuck into the room, there was Jorge in bed and alone. Luck was on my side. We stealthily made our way to his bed, grabbed him by his hair, and smacked him hard in the throat with the blackjack to prevent him from calling out to the guards. We then grabbed a lamp and yanked out the cord, using it to bind and hog-tie his hands and feet behind him. We gagged him with a sock I found on the floor. Once we had him gagged and tied, I went to work getting him to tell me the combo for the huge safe in his bedroom. I knew he had something of mine, and that was where I would find it. It took some... convincing, but he finally gave me the combo before I stuffed the sock back into his mouth. When I opened the safe, I spotted what I had come for. My bag was sitting there, and I could see that nothing was even unpacked from it yet. I noticed that not only my money was in the safe but also other valuables that were now mine.

I quickly removed my money bag and the other loot and slammed the safe shut. Spinning on my heels and returning back the way we came in, I could hear Jorge yelling at me through his gag. I couldn't make out the words, but I could guess what he was saying. I smirked and turned back to him as I whacked him with the blackjack once more and grabbed the ropes that got us in there and would now get us the hell out.

"No one gets to fuck with my money, Jorge, you sorry sack of shit. I got what's mine plus a little interest. Don't fucking come after me or try to contact me again, or you *will* be sorry."

With that, we used the ropes to scale down the building to the ground where our van waited. My crew had already made their way back down and waited for me, eager to get the fuck out of there before we were caught. Leaving the ropes behind, we ran to the van and jumped in, yelling for Pat, the driver, to get the fuck out of there as I pulled the door closed.

We drove like a bullet train for the border. Once we crossed that, we knew we'd be safe. But we had to make it that far before we could stop to catch our breath and to throw Jorge's guy out on the side of the street still hog-tied It was a wild adventure, a life-or-death situation, and through it all, I never lost focus. I got my money back like I said I would, and that was all that mattered.

CHAPTER 7

RISE OF THE EMPIRE

After that last failed trip to Mexico to procure the ever-elusive cartel connection that wasn't going to rob or kill me, I decided it was best to sit on that idea for a while. The summer was almost over, and weed was slowly trickling back into the city. But the experience really stayed with me.

I had always thought that once I got to the top of that mountain, I would get out and go legit. My first business was a lucrative real estate development company. It did very well from the start, and I loved building it up and seeing it succeed.

Next, I started a high-end car dealership when I was twenty-seven or twenty-eight. This attracted more legitimate business from professional athletes, politicians, movie stars, news celebrities, and of course strippers looking to spend cash.

I was good friends with most of the strippers in the area and dated a lot of them, too. Those ladies knew how to have a good time.

One hot afternoon, a platinum-blonde stripper named Nancy came into the dealership. "Hi, Jimmy!" she cooed at me. "You told me you could help me out if my credit was bad, and I really need a car." She pulled out a bag full of bills. My mind started to spin, contemplating how I might finance this girl's nice car and keep it off the books with a cash sale. I helped Nancy buy a Mercedes Coup with all the extras. She winked her heavy eyelashes and strutted out, wagging her full hips at me suggestively as she left.

Before long, I was helping all the strippers out with new rides. Those women typically had terrible credit but lots of cash. They pranced into the dealership in their high heels, short skirts, and plunging necklines with their purses stuffed full of cash, looking to buy the hottest cars they could to drive around town and attract tipping customers to their establishments.

One time, an especially lovely stripper named Lucille came in near closing time, and our business conversation got a little—well—heated. It was rowdy, for sure, but not in an angry way. She wanted to buy a Bugatti on the showroom floor. The car was sexy, but as we talked about its many fine features and selling points, we kept getting distracted by each other. Lucille certainly had plenty of fine features of her own. We wound up in my office doing a steamy little strip number in private.

The car dealership was the perfect cross-over to acquire high-paying clients for my drug business. It was a plush, upscale dealership specializing in exotic and luxury cars, and it flourished. My clientele included all of the most elite people from all over the country.

Around that same time, blow entered the drug scene. It was everywhere—and I mean everywhere. Everyone was doing it—all the rich people, the poor people, the middle class, and even the people you wouldn't expect. It was a big part of the cool scene and the way to be at the time. The "upper crust" was highly involved.

Two of my big-time clients were top neurosurgeons in the Chicago area and were known worldwide for their surgical skills. They each easily spent a million a year just to feed their party habits. I learned at a young age that whether it was marijuana, prescription meds, cocaine, alcohol, speed, Xanax, ecstasy, nicotine, or whatever a person desired, drugs were an unspoken fact of life. I knew that people would get it from some-one else if they didn't get it from me. Nothing would stop people from wanting to party. I figured if these successful people who were twice my age lived their lives that way, who was I to tell them to stop?

I had the perfect cover and drove exotic cars all the time. My dad had been the driving instructor for the police and fire academy in Illinois. He was voted the best driver in Illinois for years because of his outstanding skill. I learned from him, and he was the best. Even so, I expanded my driving skill later on by attending Corvette and Ferrari racecar driving schools in Arizona. They taught me to race on hot tracks, and they'd pour oil all over the track to spin my car out. I had to learn to regain control and drive out of it. They taught stunt driving and all sorts of cool and risky maneuvers. I became an expert.

My weed and blow customers also purchased luxury cars. I had a unique dealer plate number allotted to my dealership, and I only allowed a handful of my top guys to drive my dealership cars. It was so cool to go to the top-rated clubs in Chicago at night and see a special, roped-off, VIP parking section housing all of my dealership cars bearing the same plate number parked in a line. It was a beautiful sight. Of course, I was a VIP at every club, restaurant, and strip club in the city because all the club owners were buying their products from me—cars and houses, too.

Later on, I bought a strip club. The club had multiple uses. It was a great place to meet my crew and discuss business without eyes or ears on us. If we didn't meet at the club, we met at the dealership. The girls were good at knowing if their customers needed anything to make the night better for their bachelor parties or whatever else brought them to our establishment.

When all the famous Rush and Division Street nightclubs in downtown Chicago closed or slowed down in the early hours of the morning, everyone who was anyone would show up at my brownstone in the city's elite Gold Coast. I had a knack for bringing people together and was well-known for my famous parties. They were my escape from the pressures of running my legal and illegal businesses. I shielded my dual identity, even at those world-class parties I held between all my other wild life-or-death adventures. I never dealt directly with buyers, and no one but my own crew knew I was in charge of the whole empire. Some people may have suspected I was the man behind the curtain, but I was careful to keep those people guessing.

I had some of today's most famous stars at my parties before they were famous. I had all the local celebrities, top politicians, doctors, most elite athletes, lawyers, porn stars, and countless beautiful women. I had an incredible swimming pool and a cozy pool table room with three tables, pinball, and various other arcade games and machines. We enjoyed betting on long pool tournaments and championships.

My friend Dawn owned a place called Vogue Fashions, and she employed over a hundred women all the time. They did lingerie fashion shows, but mainly they were high-class escorts, and eventually, almost all of them worked at my strip club. Dawn always came to my famous brownstone parties with a whole fleet of beautiful women. This made all the rich guy's clamor to attend.

Dawn herself is a unique character and still one of my best friends. Dawn was the "madam of all madams" and was arrested many times, but she beat all her cases in the Chicago State courts. The press and media dubbed her "The Teflon Dawn." After winning all her state cases and trials, Dawn was arrested on federal charges, lost that case, and was sentenced and sent to the same prison at the same time as Martha Stewart. My parties certainly never ran short on unique and interesting people.

Around the same time my business hit a plateau, I finally made my cartel connection: Alberto Pedro Gonzalez—a narco trafficker in northern Mexico with a short temper, a thick Mexican accent, and a string of dead bodies—all people who'd looked at him wrong or pissed him off on a bad day. Alberto loved everything American—movies, music, and especially cars. Alberto and I shared an obsession with Corvettes. When I purchased one for myself, I would drive it for as long as I wanted and then sell it to Alberto and make a substantial profit. He sometimes bought five or ten cars from me at a time. Alberto's location near the Mexican-Arizona border made his place just a short trip from our Arizona property.

Richie had made the connection. He was trying to make up for his other fuck-ups in the business. He had introduced me to Alberto at a famous nightclub in Arizona. With Alberto supplying the business, there was no stopping me. We had to be smart because law enforcement had seen the huge surge of products coming into Illinois and neighboring states. They wanted a bust. The DEA, the FBI, and local authorities all had their eyes on Chicago.

Before sunrise one Sunday, the phone rang. I let it ring for what seemed ten minutes straight before I got up and answered it.

"This better be good."

"Hello, my friend Jimmy."

"Alberto? What's up?" Alberto wasn't the kind of guy to just call and say "hi." My pulse quickened. So much for a lazy Sunday morning.

"Oh, not much. I have your friend here with me." I could hear a hint of sarcastic anger, which was alarming.

"My friend?" I asked, my mind racing to figure out what was going on.

"Yeah, that fucking long-haired loser you hang out with." His tone had changed. Yup, that was anger, seething and lethal like a stomped-on hornet's nest.

"I think it's been a while since we caught up. Why don't you come down here and visit." Again, his tone changed. I suddenly realized who he was talking about and that danger was imminent. I didn't flinch. One of the talents I'd developed was how to dodge and roll, not only on the sports field but in life itself. My parents told me I was born in a crossfire hurricane and always ready from a young age to roll with whatever punches came my way. Being born in Kankakee presented an overwhelming storm of adverse conditions I had to learn to deal with. And it had never let up.

"I'm on my way," I said.

"See you soon," Alberto responded coldly.

I looked over at the bed, and Brandy was lying there smiling at me. She had knockout curves and a stunning smile. Even early in the morning, she took my breath away. She turned over and opened her legs for me as her hand slid down between them.

"Sweetheart, you're killing me. You're going to hold that thought until I get back."

"Oh, come on, Jimmy. You can play for a couple of hours. She reached over and grabbed her glass of champagne. We'd only had a few hours of sleep. Between the late-night party and the fun in the sheets, it was more of a continuing night than an early morning. Brandy was amazing in bed and knew how to please me. But she was also a kind soul and had a tender heart. Fucking Richie.

I took a four-hour flight to Phoenix and picked up one of my Corvettes at the Arizona ranch. The drive through the Sonoran Desert to Alberto's would take a little while. It was silent except for the crunch of the Corvette's tires. The trip was unexpected, but I felt in control despite the threat in Alberto's voice. The rough patches on the shitty Mexican roads jostled me, but not my nerves. I enjoyed the hours on the road, despite my reason for being there.

As I drove, I thought about my dad and how he raised me like a cop—the only way he knew how. He was the best damn cop. In big ways and small ways, he raised me to take life head-on. He taught me how to keep my cool, even when everyone around me was losing theirs.

Still deep in thought, I continued to drive along. I knew these Mexican backroads well and turned onto blind intersections on the desolate roads without hesitation. Dad had taught me everything I needed to know about being a man, from how to break a tackle to how to break a man's femur to how to break a woman's heart. The hardest thing I ever did was break *his* heart.

I slowed as a Mexican narco with an AK-47 stepped into the road and broke the headlight beams splayed across the road. Then two more narcos emerged from the gloom, likewise armed to the teeth and angry—the cartel's way of life.

The one thing Big Jim didn't teach me was when to quit. I had a life I didn't want to quit, and Dad hated quitters.

The narco pointed, and I responded with a nod, turning the 'Vette up a steep, steel-gated driveway past more armed men at each switch on the flagstone ramp and continuing on until a massive pink mansion under spotlights crowning the hilltop loomed into view. More narco gunmen toting machine guns and cartridge belts were perched on the balconies. In a parapet, I spotted a sniper with a 50-cal eyeing the valley below. Alberto's gleaming collection of Corvettes (all purchased through me) lined the sprawling paved area in front of a sizable detached garage.

When to quit is one helluva hard lesson to learn. So, ask yourself this question, would you have quit any sooner?

I reached the entrance and threw the 'Vette into park. I took a deep breath through my nose, nerves steeled and senses on full alert. I approached Alberto's villa, and another narco patted me down and led me inside.

I surveyed the scene. The villa looked like a poor man's Playboy mansion. Loud norteño music echoed through the building. Flies buzzed around a huge banquet buffet that had been flipped over on the ground. Beautiful women, mostly Russian or Ukrainian and all naked or nearly so, cavorted and lounged around an Olympic-sized pool. I had seen it all before, and my mind was on my business.

The narco led me toward a doorway where I heard whimpers. At the threshold, I peered in, and the narco shoved me into the room—a kitchen—with the barrel of his AK-47.

Like the house, the kitchen was immense, like it belonged in a restaurant. In the middle of the room, I observed Richie tied to a chair, stripped and filthy and beaten to a bloody pulp. A blindfold covered his eyes.

Standing beside him with his eyes bugged out and his belly bulging was Alberto with his long ponytail and goatee. He was covered in flashy gold jewelry and dressed like he was heading to a resort dinner reservation. He was always dressed in the best clothes available.

"Fucking Jimmy! Now shall I kill him?" Alberto asked with a sneer.

Richie heard my name and yelled, "Jimmy? Man!" But Alberto grabbed Richie and rammed the gun barrel into Richie's nostrils.

Alberto raised his voice to an urgent, threatening pitch and met my gaze with wild eyes. "Know how much he stole from you and me? Over one hundred thousand."

"If that's the case, Alberto, I'll make it up to you."

Richie struggled in the chair and pled with me. "Help me, Jimmy!"

"Jimmy! You missing the point, *cabron*! It was five kilos," Alberto yelled.

Richie was panicking and started to cry. "Jimmy—JIMMY!" I lunged forward and smacked Richie hard. Damn hard. Richie began to cry even harder. "JIMMY"!

I leaned close to him. "You did this, Richie. Nobody else. Shut up, or I'll kill you myself."

Alberto laughed and put his pistol to Richie's skull. "I told you—I'm happy to kill this skinny *pendejo* for you," he said. "Right now, Jimmy. Right now!"

"Alberto, no," I said as Alberto bugged his eyes again, trying to intimidate me. It didn't work. I looked Alberto firmly in his freakish eyes and said, "You want me to do this to one of your guys, Alberto? That's the rule now? No—no, that's not the rule. The rule is, your men are your men. They mess up in the states, you deal with it. This stupid, skinny *pendejo* is *my* stupid, greedy, coke-head *pendejo*." I kicked Richie for emphasis. "I deal with it—me."

"You ain't no Superman, and this *cabron* ain't no Jimmy Olsen," Alberto said. He rammed the barrel of his pistol into Richie's mouth.

Alberto's finger tightened on the trigger. I struck like lightning, sweeping Richie's legs so hard it broke the chair legs and sent Richie crashing to the floor. Alberto's bullet pierced the nearby steel cabinet, barely missing Richie's head.

I jumped on Richie like a pit bull on a Chihuahua, hitting him. "WHY? ARE? YOU? SO! FUCKING! STUPID?"

Alberto and some of his partiers who filed into the kitchen to observe the scene began to laugh.

"Kill him, Jimmy! Kill him!" Alberto yelled.

"NOOO, noooo, noooo!" screamed Richie.

I stood up, kicking Richie one more time for effect.

"Finish him, Jimmy," said Alberto.

"He'll be taken care of when I get back home," I replied.

"Now!" Alberto insisted.

"At home," I said, continuing to untie Richie's ropes.

Alberto pointed his finger at me. "You got *huevos, cabron.*"

"Don't mess around, Alberto, and don't point that gun at me," I said continuing to untie Richie.

Alberto held his ground for a long beat and then tucked his gun away. "You are my guy, Jimmy."

"And this dirtbag is *my* guy," I said. "*Donde esta* his *ropas*?"

Gesturing to a bystander, Alberto commanded "*Ropa. Ropa! Dame tu ropa, chingada!*". A coked-up Mexican obeyed Alberto and stripped down to his briefs, holding out his clothes and offering them to me.

I took the clothes and pulled Richie to his feet to help him get dressed. He was beaten so badly he couldn't even stand.

I held out my hand to shake Alberto's hand. "I promise—if your guys screw up in the States, I deliver 'em to you. I give you my word."

Alberto eyed his own men for their reaction, then clasped hands with me. He leaned in and said, "I never want to see this skinny *pendejo* again."

"Never again," I replied.

I half dragged Richie through the motley spectators as the narcos looked on. I got Richie to the 'Vette and shoved my bloodied friend into the passenger's seat.

I started the car, emotionless, and began backing out. Richie whispered to me, "Thanks, man, for not going full Jimmy on me—"

I cut him off. "Not a word 'til we're out of here. Not a fucking word."

Richie nodded, closed his black and blue eyelids, and sobbed with relief.

I leaned into my seat and headed down the driveway as "Outlaw Man" by the Eagles played through the car speakers. I let out a long breath and thought to myself, *There's another hard lesson to learn—who you can trust. Employee, partner, mother, father, cop, governor, FBI agent, drug dealer, friend—everyone has imperfections that make them hard to trust. The sad fact is that nobody's perfect. We all have two sides. We all have things we're proud of and things we hide in order to survive. We all learn to live a life in deep cover.*

As the car roared up the dirt road, headlights roaming the desert, we headed north toward the border and to a highway miles away. Richie said, "Thanks, Jimmy. You saved my life."

"You're damn right I did—*again*! And you better never forget it either, Richie. I mean it."

That night, I learned that hard lesson about trust better than most.

Once Richie and I made it back into the U.S., I dropped him off at the ranch in Arizona, and I boarded a flight to Chicago. I got comfortable in my first-class seat, leaned back, and reflected. *How many times have I made this same flight after driving down to see Alberto in Mexico? Thank God it hasn't always been under these circumstances.*

I remembered the first time I met Alberto face to face. I'd gone to the copycat Playboy mansion on that day too, but it was bright midday. There had been a huge gourmet banquet laid out and more nude women sunbathing outside, and I'd carried a briefcase with me containing five million dollars in cold hard cash. The Chicago mafia had been getting their cocaine from Central America, but through Alberto, I could get a much better price. This made me the top man with the Chicago mob.

Carrying my briefcase, I entered a room where Alberto waited at a large table surrounded by heavily armed narcos.

"Jimmy Keene," I said.

Alberto's bulging eyes were eager but cold. "Jimmy! Jimmy Keene! You want food? You want women?"

"Business first, Alberto," I said.

"Sit." Alberto motioned to a chair, and I sat down, placing my briefcase in front of me. "Let me see."

I opened the briefcase, flush with cash, and Alberto's eyes bugged out even more.

"What will stop me from killing you now amigo, eh? I take this money and have my men chop you up and spread you all over the desert, eh?"

I stayed cool, sliding the briefcase toward Alberto.

"Here, take it. You kill me? Fine. You have five million. But think about how much we can make if we do business together and I bring you one of these cases full every month."

Alberto sat back, thinking about it. He smiled and looked at his men. "This is my guy! Jimmy, we are in business!"

I smiled from the comfort of my first-class seat, thinking to myself that Alberto was a cold-blooded killer. Who knows how many bodies he'd buried in the desert? But I had learned it took brains, not brawn, to outsmart a killer.

Back home in Chicago, I strolled out of the elevator in the parking garage at O'Hare airport just in time to see a Jaguar XJ6 gliding into a handicapped spot. The Jag's perfectly healthy driver exited the car, and I shook my head, heading to a bright yellow Lamborghini Countach. I drew something out of my pants pocket that looked like a desk pen and pressed a button on its side. The "cap" lit blue, and I swept it over the sexy fenders of the car until it flashed red. I commended myself as I pulled a small magnetic tracking device from under my car—something I was accustomed to finding—and strode toward the illegally parked Jaguar. I tucked the device inside its wheel well and returned to my car laughing quietly.

I hopped in the car and headed home, tunes cranked and the pressure off. Behind me, O'Hare glowed in the night as the jets arrived and departed. It reminded me of a huge light show.

I sighed as I thought about Richie. We went way back—friends since peewee hockey. Richie had moved into a house that I'd bought for him out in Phoenix not too far from the ranch warehouse. The warehouse was a drop house when needed, and Richie would help oversee the shipments trucked north from Mexico to Chicago. I'd warned him a million times to cut back on using dope. This time he'd gotten dangerously greedy.

Richie had a rough time growing up. His family was a train wreck, and it messed him up big time. He took to booze and weed early, like a lot of people I grew up with. That wasn't my path though. Adrenaline and money were my drugs, and they had a funny way of giving me that third thing that I craved.

I shifted the Lambo into warp speed and zoomed north to my mansion. As I wheeled the Lambo into the wide drive, my twelve-thousand-square-foot house and multi-acre property lit by landscaping lights looked like a suburban Wayne manor. Through the leaded glass of a massive door, my silhouette deactivated an alarm and I stepped inside. The place was dark. I reactivated the alarm and walked through my immense and immaculate home. The interior was masculine but clearly had the touch of female friends and a designer. In the ambient light coming through the many windows, I found my way to a wide, open staircase.

I climbed up to my bedroom and opened the door. I paused, now on alert—it had been open when I'd left home. Brandy had been here, but I didn't know why she would close it before leaving. As if pulled from thin air, I produced a Glock 20 with a chrome-ported barrel—cool, lethal. (So was the gun.)

Suddenly, I was on again. I entered the room like a detective, two-handing the pistol, and sweeping the shadows of the huge bedroom. Then I spied weak light seeping from under the bathroom door. I crept to it, and a shadow swept over the light cast below.

BOOM! I booted the door open, scaring gorgeous, olive-skinned Brandy in her negligee. She screamed. Brandy quivered like jelly as I took her into my arms, my pistol still in hand and cold through her barely-there chemise.

"God, Jimmy!" Brandy said.

"Brandy, what the hell, babe?" I replied.

"I think I just peed some more," said Brandy, breathing deliberately to slow her heartrate.

"You deserve it. Why are you here?" I asked her.

"You asked me to stay 'til you got back. I've been here more than a day waiting for you."

I squeezed her tighter, giving her a deep kiss. I hadn't expected her to take that request to heart. "I forgot. I'm sorry."

"I've been waiting forever," she replied.

"I had some business." I stopped her talking with a passionate kiss, drawing her close.

"Jimmy, put that thing away."

"Which thing?" I laughed, lifting her like nothing off the tile floor, her legs wrapping around me like they were made for me, and her succulent body pressed tightly against mine.

I carried her to the bed as Brandy stripped off my shirt, revealing my bodybuilder's eight-pack. I kicked off my shoes and took her to the bed where soft light from outside bathed the scene. I deposited the pistol on the nightstand as my muscular body engulfed her, overtaking her.

"You're such an animal," said Brandy, and I laughed, but it was muffled by her kiss as we melted into the shadows and one another.

After a few hours of rest, I rolled off the king-size bed after checking on Brandy. I picked up the cool-ass Glock and headed for the bathroom.

"When I put your shirt in the wash last night, there was blood on it," Brandy said, her eyes still closed.

I continued to the bathroom, hiding the pistol I was carrying.

All of the walls in the bathroom were mirrored, and I looked over my shoulder, on guard, and closed the door.

"I had to put a guy in his place," I said through the door, pressing a button behind the toilet tank. With the slightest click, a wide mirrored panel popped out of place, hinged like a giant medicine cabinet. "It was nothing," I continued.

"What?" said Brandy from the bedroom.

I swung open the panel, revealing a door into my secret hideaway the size of a master bedroom. Inside, was a full desk, computer, phone, an electronic scale, and a bank of CCTV monitors with a joystick feeding info back from cameras around my home and the drug warehouse.

On the south wall was a collection of guns and martial arts weaponry. Expensive paintings covered the remaining walls, and I kept a favorite collection of leather jackets inside a climate-controlled glass booth. At the far end was a huge safe.

I quickly replaced the pistol in its slot and then ducked out. As I stepped out of the secret room, I pressed the mirror shut and turned to see Brandy standing there watching the secret panel close.

"Is that why you always close the bathroom door?" she asked. I was pissed, but I covered it, flashing my million-dollar smile.

"Why do you ask so many questions?" I asked. Brandy looked puzzled, but her expression cleared as I grabbed her, wrestling her toward my six-person shower. I threw on the water, which doused us as we laughed and kissed.

CHAPTER 8

WHAT WE ALWAYS FEARED

In 1992, Tim and I were busted for possession of marijuana. We were having the product shipped through a regular shipping company in refrigerator boxes from the Arizona warehouse. If we were receiving a huge shipment, we would wait and watch for the commercial truck to deliver it. They would stack the boxes on our designated shipping dock and leave. Once they left, we would wait a little longer and see if any cops showed up. If they didn't, we would load everything up on a new truck and take it to another warehouse. We would change the location for each shipment so no two were ever shipped to the same address.

After one such delivery, we had finished loading everything and were on our way to the local warehouse. Tim was driving the larger truck, and I was behind acting as a lookout in my Chevy 4x4. Snow dusted down around us, and there were enough cars on the road that the crawling traffic had clogged to a halt. Despite the standstill, I stayed alert. Suddenly, I glanced in my rearview mirror and spotted several long-haired men with guns crouching and darting quickly toward us through the motionless traffic.

"Shit." At first, I thought it was a hit. Then I glimpsed a half-hidden flash of metal—a badge. It was a sting. I looked up in front of us, and several more men approached from both directions toward Tim's truck.

A moment later, several cops had guns drawn and pointed at the driver's side of the truck. A few more men were preparing to open the back, and two more were coming around the other side. Tim cooperated and slowly got out with his palms raised above his head.

I automatically held my hands up when the cops coming from behind reached my tailgate. Two more police from the front trained their guns on me and told me to get out. As I opened the door, I saw the cops slash the tops of the boxes in the truck with a box cutter.

"We got it! It's here," one of them yelled.

The officers stuffed Tim and me into the back of a squad car and drove to the station. I was calm on the outside, but inside my gut twisted. It was one thing for me to get arrested, but Tim was here by my side. He was always willing to help, and I relied on him, but he was also my little brother whom I fiercely protected and tried to keep out of harm's way. I felt I had failed him. I also knew I had failed my father.

When I got my one phone call, I called my girlfriend at home.

"Hey, listen—I'm not coming home tonight."

"What? What's wrong?" April asked.

"It's what we always feared," I said and hung up.

April knew what this meant. She ran into the bedroom and pulled up the floorboards just under the rug. She took out the two kilos and 150 grand I'd stashed there and put it in a laundry basket under some clothing. She carried it out to the car and left. As she pulled away, an unmarked police car followed her, but she turned down a side street and drove fast enough to lose it. She jumped out of her car and ran into a neighbor's yard. It was snowing heavily now, and it blanketed everything. She threw the two kilos into some pine trees and took off. When she turned onto the main street three blocks away from the house, several cop cars tore past in the opposite direction. She'd barely made it out of there.

A short while later, April knocked on my dad's door. When Big Jim answered, she handed him the basket and looked him directly in the face.

"Jimmy's in trouble. He needs you."

Tim and I had a great lawyer that got us off on a technicality. When a narcotic squad is pumped up about all the rewards and press surrounding a large bust, sometimes they screw up how the shit rolls downhill, and they get their asses handed to them. They knew the marijuana was ours, but they failed to pin it on us because they didn't do their job right. That really put a bee in their bonnet. Law enforcement realized then that we were not small-time peddlers, even if they couldn't prove it, and that painted a larger target on our backs.

When I went to see my dad, he'd already heard the news and knew we'd been released.

I walked into the house after a brief knock and found him sitting in his chair. Tears gathered in his eyes as he looked at me. I felt guilt, shame, and sadness.

"I'm sorry, Dad."

"I never wanted this for you, son—not for either of you. You had so much going for you. You could have been a pro ball player by now and left this hellhole." He trailed off and hung his head like he was to blame. Somehow, my father felt responsible for my choices.

"Dad, playing ball was never for me." I loved football, and I meant it. For years after I stopped, I still felt minor pain from old sports injuries. I'd seen my friends sustain serious concussions and break bones. Playing professional ball would have been a short career, and then I would have suffered the crippling physical results of hard play for the rest of my life.

Dad just shook his head. "So, were you ever working in the stock market? I should have asked more questions—I should have—" He didn't finish the sentence.

I told him everything then. It was one of the hardest things I've ever had to do. To look into his eyes and see such disappointment from my hero was heartbreaking. But when I finished, all I could see there was love and forgiveness.

When Mom found out, she was furious with me for getting Tim involved in my dealings. She also lashed out at my father for being so lenient with us when we were growing up. I knew this was her way of showing she was scared, worried, and loved us, but it always came out as a scolding. I never got back the money that April took over there that day. I never asked my dad what happened to it.

Before that incident, I honestly hadn't worried much about cops. I felt we were one step ahead of them and always playing it cool. I even had several law enforcement officers on the payroll—guys I had grown up with. They would give me a heads-up if the Feds were in town so I could lie low for a few months. I was usually more concerned about getting shot in the face by an angry drug lord.

I still hadn't reached the top of that mountain yet, and I couldn't let this bust stop me. I convinced myself that we just had to be more careful, tighten the ranks, and be more elusive. And that strategy worked—for four more years.

A few months later, I got a call from my good friend T-Roy. T-Roy and I had grown up and played ball together since we were five. T-Roy and Big Reg were tight. We'd all stayed close over the years. T-Roy had become a leader of one of the Black gangs in south Chicago about ten years prior. He was one of my top distributors in South Side and made it possible for my crew and me to frequent that part of the city without getting killed or attacked.

Once a few years back, T-Roy had proven his friend-ship by helping Tim and me out of a tough spot in South Side. We'd arranged to meet a client there, but some South Side gang members showed up and threatened to kill us on the spot just for being there. We'd been surrounded by a group of hulking, menacing guys all holding guns on us and looking more than happy to pull some triggers. We put our hands up slowly.

"We're not looking for trouble. Just here to do busi-ness," I said.

A small but wiry man wearing a sinister sneer strode to stand in front of us. He was clearly the leader of the group—the type who didn't look like much and knew he had to make up for his lack of physical strength with razor-sharp wits and an even sharper reputation. "You got no *business* on our turf, fools. Looks like you just made a very bad decision, and now it's *us* who'll be taking care of business."

I maintained my cool demeanor, but inside, I started to worry. I didn't see a good way out of this. Then, I spotted T-Roy approaching from behind the guy. T-Roy met my eyes briefly, passing a silent message to let him handle it. He talked down the leader of the group with calm collection.

"Hey, man. This here's Jimmy and Timmy Keene. They're cool. Let 'em go."

The small man looked incredulous. "What for? What's so cool about these clowns?"

"They're quick. They're sharp—the kind of guys that'll be useful for us to keep in touch with. They've got connections. Trust me." The guy listened to T-Roy, and we got out of there without becoming the subjects of target practice.

The front bathroom in our elementary school was just the same as South Side Chicago—if you weren't from there and took a turn that landed you in the wrong part of town, bad things happened. That was simply the law of life there. T-Roy spoke with me about that incident later, wondering why the hell I'd shown up there in the first place. "Man, Jimmy. You've always been fearless to a fault," he'd said, shaking his head.

I'd smiled back at him. "Yeah, maybe so. But it worked out for the better, didn't it?" T-Roy helped me build strong connections in South Side after that.

Back in my brownstone, T-Roy's voice sounded deadly serious through the phone receiver. "Hey,

Jimmy, we got a problem," T-Roy said after briefly catching up on friends and family.

"What is it?"

"It's your boy Richie. He's into us bad. It's really making me look bad to the other guys. They know he's a friend of yours, but if it was anyone else, he would be taken out by now."

Richie! Fucking Richie again!

Richie O'Reilly was always a major thorn in my side, even though I loved the guy. The trouble he put me through never seemed to end. I had decided Richie lacked any shred of common sense—just a natural-born fuck-up.

Richie had gotten himself in deep with the South Side gang's gambling ring to the tune of eighty-two thousand dollars. I knew Richie was an idiot, but I was still shocked to hear that. Even someone like Richie knew you didn't fuck with these people. If you wanted to gamble, you only gambled with the money you had. If they gave you a front, the interest would be so high that the only way to pay it off would be in the back-street with a bullet through your head.

"It's my crew over in south Lake Shore," T-Roy explained. "And those cats just don't give a shit. He's in trouble, Jimmy. He's gotta have the money tonight before midnight, or they're going to cut his balls off and stuff them down his throat before putting a bullet in his skull."

I knew T-Roy wasn't exaggerating. The Black gangs of South Side Chicagoland were vicious and handled such matters with grim, businesslike finality.

"They only want to deal with you," T-Roy added.

"I'll take care of it. Thanks, T-Roy, for the heads-up."

"No problem, man. It's what friends do."

I hung up the phone and groaned. *Here I go again— heading into an unknown situation with dangerous people to save Richie's ass! One of these days, he's going to get himself or both of us killed. How much more of this do I have to take? He just doesn't learn.*

A little while later, I rolled out of the parking lot of a stash house with a satchel full of "save Richie" money and drove toward the South Side. I squeezed my hands around the steering wheel like a boa constrictor suffocating its prey. My adrenaline revved, and my senses heightened in anticipation.

When I arrived at the old warehouse that had been converted into a party pad and a convenient place for backroom poker games, several gang members stood outside. I parked the car and strode confidently toward the door. One of the guys nodded his head and pointed to the side of the building. I detoured to the side and saw a few more guys posted at another door. I entered and found a staircase going down. I descended purposefully, and at the bottom, there was Richie with his arms tied together and looped over a water pipe on the ceiling. He had just enough slack to touch the floor with his toes. His face was black and blue.

"I'm here with his money," I said to no one in particular.

"Hear that? Jimmy Keene is here to save your ass," one of the men said and slammed his knuckles into Richie's ribs.

Another man strolled over to me holding a ledger, and I scanned it. It was clear Richie's gambling was an ongoing issue. Richie had been gambling here for months. He had some wins but mostly losses, and he'd been in their debt—plus interest—for weeks now.

"You know this boy is only alive because he's yours, right? I don't want him here no more. If I see him, I'll kill him myself."

"Understood." I reached into my bag, grabbed the freshly wrapped piles of bills, and handed them over.

By this time, they had cut Richie down and were carrying him over to where I stood. He could hardly walk. It felt like déjà vu. So many times, since we were kids, we had been in this same situation—Richie doing stupid shit, and me bailing him out. Enough was enough.

As we got in the car to leave, Richie glanced over at me as if he were ready to say something. He took one look at my stony expression and decided against it. We drove the rest of the way to his apartment in silence.

As I got him settled, I still couldn't speak to him. I left without uttering a word.

I drove back to my place still tense from the whole experience. The tight muscles in my shoulders and upper back felt as hard and solid as granite boulders. Thankfully, I was having a brownstone party that night, and that would allow me to put all of my concerns about Richie out of my mind. I needed those parties to unwind after days as bad as this one had been.

When I arrived at the house, loud music blared through the building, and it was full of people. Men and scantily dressed women danced holding drinks, laughing, and thoroughly enjoying themselves. Several of the girls came my way and greeted me as I passed.

"It's about time you showed up, Jimmy. Wouldn't be much of a party without you."

"There you are stranger! Save me a dance later, okay?"

One woman brushed her fingers along my taught shoulders, and her fingers lingered for a moment to knead the skin around the base of my neck. "Geez, Jimmy, was it a bad day? I can help you let go of some of that tension in a little while." She handed me a drink and winked back at me, her gaze holding mine steadily through lowered lashes as she strolled away down the hall toward the pool table room.

I smiled back at her. I liked the sound of that offer. For now, I took a steady draw from the cup she'd handed me and strolled through the brownstone letting the jovial, upbeat atmosphere wash over me. Several people played a raucous card game at a nearby table. Men draped their arms around their women, both absorbed in each other and intoxicated by the rich, heady environment I'd created. I could hear people laughing around the pool, and a handful of gorgeous girls ran past to join the fun wearing next to nothing. People lounged on the luxurious, designer furniture in rooms illuminated with soft mood lighting. Other rooms were bright and teeming with energy. There was something for everyone here. I didn't use any of the products I provided other people with, but this scene was what I craved—the luxury, the carefree abandon, and the connections with important people from all different backgrounds. I loved having this place to bring them all under one roof, and I loved being the lynchpin that held this magnificent scene together.

Later that year, spring was turning to summer, and Lake Michigan's beaches were full of locals taking advantage of the break from the harsh Chicago winter. Kevin had returned from his time in the Navy, and I'd put him in charge of security, the Chicago North Side, and the Milwaukee territory. He was still sometimes stationed at the naval base in Great Lakes, Illinois, and had deep connections to the Milwaukee mob. After his naval training, Kevin was even more crazy and lethal than before. He praised himself as an underwater demolition man, and for good reason. Kevin was also in charge of collection and security for my operations. You didn't want to be stuck owing money when Kevin came to collect.

We had been dealing with some radical renegade cowboys from Milwaukee for several years who owned a top-rated strip club there. They would either drive their boats down and meet us on Lake Michigan to make transactions, or Kevin and Big Bryan would go up to Milwaukee and meet them at their club. That spring, since the weather was clearing up, Kevin decided to deliver the five-kilo shipment to their club in person.

As Kevin and Big Bryan climbed out of the car, several masked men with guns closed in and held them up. They tied Kevin and Bryan up and stole the product. After they left, Kevin was able to reach his pocketknife, and he used it to slice through the ropes holding him. Once freed, they paid a visit inside the club. Kevin told the club owner who was there that day what had happened, and he was surprised when the man acted oblivious to the whole incident. The club owner said the cameras weren't working, so there was nothing they could use to identify the men.

Even though Kevin had been dealing with this guy for years, something didn't feel right. Kevin wasn't about to ask me to write it off as a loss—not Kevin. He was like a pit bull with a bone. He just wouldn't let it slide. About a year later, he heard rumors of someone bragging about the score. When he started asking questions, the answers all pointed back to the club owner.

One night we were all out on the town at a club, and Kevin spotted one of the Milwaukee club owner's main guys—a guy named Devon. He and Big Bryan grabbed Devon and took him into a back room. Kevin laid into him, and Devon finally confessed the whole story. The club owners had set it up, and the one they'd spoken with that night had watched on the cameras as Kevin and Big Bryan were robbed. Then the owner had lied and pretended not to know a thing. None of them knew how vengeful Kevin was when he felt wronged or to what lengths he would go to make things right.

At this point, the Milwaukee club was ready for its next shipment, so Kevin made Devon call and tell the owners that we had gotten the new shipment for a phenomenal price and that they should double their order. Devon said the product was going fast and that they needed to jump on it. Devon also said he was planning to stay in Chicago with a girl he met, and he would meet them on the waterways after the exchange was made.

Kevin started to hatch his plan. Bryan, Kevin, Big Reg, and I planned to meet the men on our boat, but when the Milwaukee guys showed up, I looked around for Kevin and couldn't find him.

"Where's Kevin?" I asked Big Bryan.

"Didn't you see him? He was all dressed up in his underwater gear a few minutes ago," Bryan said, scanning the boat, his hand shielding his eyes from the water's glare.

I knew Kevin was up to something.

Kevin was under the Milwaukee crew's boat. He was using the underwater demolition skills he'd gained as a Navy SEALs to damage the boat just enough that it would begin to take on water. He used a tool to puncture and scrape the bottom of the boat so it would respond as if it had bottomed out.

As soon as we made the transaction, the men from Milwaukee jumped back into their boat and started the engine to leave. Of course, the pressure of the boat picking up speed caused it to take on more water, and about one hundred yards away, it slowly started to sink.

We called over to them and asked what was wrong. They said their boat was sinking.

One of my guys called the harbor patrol to let them know a boat was in serious trouble. When the Milwaukee men saw the harbor patrol coming, they knew they were in trouble and dumped the drugs overboard. But Kevin had wrapped them so tightly, they were completely waterproof and floated away easily. He gathered up the packages and brought them over to our boat.

"Nothing is ever a write-off on my watch," Kevin said, grinning from ear to ear as he handed up the bags and climbed aboard.

"Great work. Let's get out of here." It was a lovely day. The warm wind off the water whipped around us, and the sun warmed our backs, but even the pleasant weather didn't compare to the sweet payback we'd just enjoyed.

Despite the arrest the year before, life was still going great. I had successful businesses, loads of money, beautiful women to keep me company, a fleet of cars, several houses, my brownstone with my famous parties, the most loyal friends I could ask for, and a great future ahead of me—and I had only just turned thirty. But that was all about to change.

CHAPTER 9

OPERATION SNOWPLOW

Over the years, I was aware that narcotic task forces were following and surveilling me. They frequently put bugs and tracking devices on my cars and on my phone, and there was a steady barrage of narcs trying to set me up. I never knew who was up to what day to day, but I always evaded those dangers with the help of friends in law enforcement who tipped me off about what they were planning. I also had close friends who kept their ears to the ground and monitored the inside whispers of the crime world. They kept me up on who had been busted and who was likely a rat.

I used anti-surveillance equipment to aid me as well, like the pen that scanned my car for tracking devices and bugs. I put heat sensors on my phones to alert me when there was more than one other party on my phone lines. I installed heat sensors above the doors in my home to detect whether someone was wearing a wire or any kind of bug. I was always careful.

Back in the eighties, Ronald Reagan issued the Anti-Drug Abuse Act. But most of it focused on cracking down on overseas drugs coming into the country and didn't affect me—at least not yet. My product didn't come in via Columbia and Panama through Florida, so I was oblivious to most of the impact. These laws were meant to cripple elusive mafia crime syndicates, but the aftermath swept up a lot of other people as well.

When law enforcement could not stop major cartel suppliers from bringing in drugs, they cracked down hard on small-time dealers and users and sent thousands of people to prison for minor drug offenses. Even someone with a clear record who had only been caught in possession of drugs once could be pegged with a mandatory minimum sentence if they'd been found with a certain amount, or if anyone testified that the offender had been planning to distribute it. Mandatory minimums meant that no matter the particular circumstances, an offender *had* to meet the minimum sentence, and parole was not an option.

The Feds used conspiracies in order to add larger drug quantities through hearsay witness testimony and increase small drug offenders' sentences. The conspiracy laws were very easy to maliciously manipulate, and those sorts of testimonies often added extreme amounts of prison time to what would have been much shorter sentences. It didn't seem like it should be legal. When someone was arrested for a small crime, prosecutors would use that person as a hearsay witness against someone else, and that hearsay witness could lie or say anything they wanted to secure a better deal even if their information was false or inaccurate. Then, that testimony would count against the other conspirators in the conspiracy trial. You couldn't beat hearsay testimony.

Sometime in October, Richie called me from a payphone, his voice hot with panic.

"Jimmy, I met up with Brandy, your old flame, and I bought some coke from her."

"Yeah, and?" I didn't see what all that had to do with me.

"I was driving my girlfriend's car, and I got pulled over. I had the coke in the trunk—I was smart—but they impounded the car." He paused, and I could hear the tension through the silence. "Man, I swear to God they're after you!"

His urgency did little to excite me. I didn't take it to heart. It was another Richie dilemma, and I was accustomed to those. Richie had been living at my house and was a hot mess like usual. Over the years, I had pulled many of Richie's business responsibilities out of his control because of his chronic drug use and irresponsibility. There were reasons I'd still never touched the stuff myself. The life I led provided me with enough of a high as it was, and I had plenty of responsibilities.

Even as messed up as Richie was, I just couldn't hang him out to dry, so I always stepped in and saved him from his own shit. I had survived a whole lot of crazy by this point, but I didn't realize how my propensity to step in on Richie's behalf would come back to haunt me. Dealing with him and all of his fuck ups was a pain in my ass, but it seemed like a harmless thing, considering the hazards of my occupation.

One cold November night in 1996 proved me wrong. I had just returned from a business trip to California and was exhausted from the travel. I pulled my car into the garage and went inside to eat and unwind. As I prepared my food in the kitchen, I heard a strange rattling coming from my front door as if someone were checking to see if it was locked. It was. It was a big house, so I wasn't sure what the noise had been. It had only lasted for a second, so I dismissed it.

I brought my food into the front room on a nice tray to watch TV as I ate. I sat down to relax, and I heard the strange rattling again. I looked at the door, but all seemed normal. Then, there was a deafening crash and a bang. It was the Feds. They hit the door with a ram, and the door exploded off the hinges. A whole squad of federal agents dressed in black swarmed into the house with guns pointing every direction. They located me immediately, the red dot sights of their automatic rifles landing all over me like a swarm of angry bees. I put my hands up and gave them no reason to fire. I had at least twelve guns pointed at my head.

"Who are you? Show me your ID or a search warrant," I demanded firmly as they threw me on the ground and held me there. Then they hoisted me up and dragged me back into the kitchen, where they handcuffed me behind my back to a chair. The guy in charge strolled up.

"Who are you? Show me your ID," I said again to the commanding officer.

"Okay, boys—search every inch of this place until we find what we're looking for." He stared me straight in the eyes.

He pulled out his ID and a copy of the search warrant and put them up to my face—so close I couldn't read them anyway.

"We're the DEA, motherfucker. We're your worst nightmare."

When the DEA does a search, they really don't care if they break, scratch, or dent anything. They don't care how much something costs. Their behavior all depends on how well you're cooperating or even what mood they may be in at any given time.

My longtime friend Maria would come over to the house and give me and my crew haircuts before we went out on the town once or twice a month, or whenever my hair needed to be cut and styled. She was the best in the city, and I wouldn't let anyone else touch my hair. I built a small salon in the basement of the house just for her so we could still play pool, party, and enjoy the time while each of us was getting our cuts.

When the DEA came back upstairs and bagged a small packet of cocaine, I knew what it was. I always had a small bit down there in the salon for those times just for Maria because she always demanded a little bump to get in the mood to do all our hair.

"Where's the rest of it, Keene? It must be somewhere."

"I don't know what you're talking about," I said, with total indifference and nonchalance.

Another agent came in holding two small .25-caliber guns. Those guns were so small they could fit in the palm of your hand. He showed them to me and set them on the kitchen table. "These yours?" He said with a smirk and a chuckle.

"No, they're a friend's. She just moved here back from California. She's staying with me for a while. But I'm sure they're registered."

Then I saw them carting things toward the front door. I had a massive collection of music—hundreds of rare, vintage collectible records, CDs, and eight-track tapes including nearly every one-hit wonder in music history.

"What the hell are you doing with my music collection? Those aren't illegal!"

"We have a right to take anything of value that may have been related to your drug business, Keene. Once this is over, you'll get it all back."

None of this made sense to me at all. All they had was a tiny bag of coke and a couple of guns that didn't belong to me, but they continued to search and tear the house apart.

The supervising federal agent and several other agents in charge stayed in the kitchen with me. The supervising agent's phone rang. He ducked around the corner to answer, but I could hear him talking.

"In the master bath. A switch next to and underneath the toilet. Got it."

He left several of his guys with me, and everyone else left.

My pulse quickened. *What the fuck? Did I hear what I thought I heard? How the fuck do they know where to look for the switch for my saferoom? Nobody knows about that except Tim, who helped me build it! This is insane.*

Several minutes later, the supervisor came in and asked me for the combination to the safe in my safe room. I could see some officers bagging up another small bag of weed along with an electric scale. They also found my 9mm Glock in the safe room, which I told them was registered as well. Another agent was nearby in the kitchen riffling through a large box of photographs.

"Hey, Jack! Look at this!" He showed a Polaroid to his supervisor.

"Is that Samantha Strong the famous porn star?" The supervisor showed me the picture.

"Damn it, those are private," I objected. "You can't go through my private pictures!" The box held some very intimate images of several different girls I'd dated in the past.

"This isn't just a public picture—do you know her?"

"It's none of your business, but yeah. She was my girlfriend for a long time."

"Here's some news, asshole. We can do whatever the fuck we want. You're a criminal. We found drugs and a scale in your house. And when we get in that safe, I'm sure we'll find more."

As he said that, another agent came in with a blow torch and headed to the bedroom. It took them over an hour, but they did get into the safe where I kept business documents, important personal documents, and 250 grand.

An agent rummaging through the kitchen pulled out a brand new five-pound bag of sugar, brought it over, and dropped it on the counter right in front of me. "What's this?" he said with a smug look on his face.

I looked at him like he was crazy. "Uh, cane sugar. It says so right on the label."

"We'll see about that! Bag it and tag it."

I shook my head thinking they must be insane, desperate, or planting something on me.

In their mind, they had connected the dots, but they needed more. For another hour, K9 dogs searched through the house for drugs. Nothing else showed up.

They kept me handcuffed to that chair in the kitchen for over twenty-four hours, demanding more information. They were certain they would find more money and dope than they did. They tried everything to intimidate me into telling them where it was. Years later when I finally sold that house, they came in with a federal forensics crew before the new owners took possession and dug up the whole yard with bulldozers and an excavation crew looking for what they would never find—buried money or drugs. Pauly, Kevin, Tim, and I enjoyed watching the whole thing from my car parked across the street.

They also started pushing me hard to tell them who my customers were and to disclose my connections to the mob and cartel. They could ask all they wanted, but I would never break trust with anyone I did business with like that—ever. No matter what, I wouldn't snitch or inform on someone who trusted me. It wasn't how I was made.

Once they figured that out, they asked for the keys to my beautiful, tricked-out Chevy 4x4. They impounded it on the basis that they suspected I'd been running drugs with it—never to be seen again. The last thing that the supervisor said to me was, "You should work with us. We have something else big on you. You should cooperate and make it easy on yourself." And they left.

Wow! I thought. *These guys are really playing hardball. The Feds are no joke. They're not as cool with me as the local police have always been. But seriously—how bad could it be? A little weed, a little blow—the guns are registered and legal. The money is legally accounted for through my businesses. What's this big thing they seem to think they have on me?*

The Feds weren't able to pin enough on me to take me into custody, but they had set their sights on me. Over the next two months, either the DEA or FBI frequently stopped by to speak with me. They kept asking questions about connections I had and pressuring me for information—anything. They were thirsty for more.

In January, I was indicted and booked. They charged me with possession with intent to distribute and possession of weapons. The gun charges were dropped because my friend who owned them presented proof of registration. It took six months to get the lab results back on the cane sugar they were testing for cocaine. I was worried that they had possibly planted something in there to frame me with. But that finally came back negative as well.

When I heard the loud knock, I knew immediately it was the police. I knew if I took the time to get dressed, they would bash my door down again, so I answered it in my boxers. There were two FBI agents and behind them were five police officers. There was a blizzard outside.

"Are you James Keene?" asked the agent in front. They must formally ask you to identify yourself first before they're allowed to arrest you. They put it on your record.

"You know who I am. You've come here enough times over the last few months," I said as I finished eating my protein bar.

"Are you James Keene?" The agent demanded again in a stern voice.

"Yes, I'm James Keene." I knew what was happening. They came in and started to cuff me.

"Can I at least get dressed? It's colder than a witch's tit out there, and I'm in my underwear. It'd be nice to have some clothes on." Three of the officers followed me up to my bedroom, and I got dressed for this next adventure.

They took me to a large general pop room that they call a drunk tank. There were over a hundred people in there. I didn't see anyone I knew personally, but I knew some of them by reputation. The ones I knew about were small-time drug dealers on the South Side. I did recognize one face. He walked up to me with panic in his eyes—fucking Richie!

We found an empty space by a wall and sat down. As soon as we got comfortable, Richie started in.

"Oh my God, Jimmy, what're we gonna do? They're gonna put us away for a long time. I can't go to prison." He kept on crying and whining.

"Shut the fuck up, man," I said. "Look over there." I gestured to some surveillance equipment in the corner. "They have bugs and cameras everywhere. Just shut the fuck up. You don't want to look weak in front of these guys, either. Never show you're afraid, or worse things will happen! Got it?"

"Yeah, man. You're right, Jimmy." Richie wiped the snot from his nose with his sleeve.

What I didn't know at the time was that this was a mass operation the Feds called Operation Snowplow. They were using informants to gather evidence about and build conspiracy cases against people selling or buying drugs. It was like a domino effect, and all of us in here had one person in common—one snitch who had ratted on several of us. Then some of those people had snitched on several more until the cops had followed the threads of information down to string us all together and net us like a school of quick and slippery fish.

The room was frigid, and the cops don't make you comfortable. When you wanted to sleep, you just rolled up a coat or shirt or whatever you had and made the best of it. We were there overnight.

We all went to an arraignment hearing the next morning at the Federal Courts building. The guards escorted us by name order to the transport bus. Once they put us on the bus, they placed Richie in the seat next to me. I thought that was strange. Richie's name order was nowhere near mine on the list. Once Richie was handcuffed and seated, he started in again.

"Jimmy, I'm losing it. What are they gonna to do with us, man? What are we going to do?"

"Shut the fuck up," I said, silencing him with a forceful gaze. I pointed to a camera wired for sound and video placed right above our heads. "Look," I said simply. I wondered how much more stupid Richie could get. I didn't think even he was that dumb. It was obvious the Feds were hoping that Richie and I would talk during the drive and spill inside information. Richie finally fell silent. It was a long, quiet drive.

Two days later, I had my bond hearing. This was the first time I had ever seen U.S. Attorney Larry Beaumont. He was cocky and, like a shark, he smelled blood in the water—he was going to do whatever it took to make an example out of me. He knew I had the money to post even a high bail amount, but he wanted me to stay in jail until my trial. As I sat and waited for them to call my name, I started noticing old girlfriends of mine coming in. They all smiled or waved. *What the fuck are you up to, Beaumont?*

There were only a couple of other people going in front of the judge for bond proceedings. The rest of the courtroom was filled with women I had known intimately or had been friends with over the years. The whole back of the courtroom was full of press. I could see the women looking at each other. Some were being catty to one another, and others were just waiting impatiently to get the whole thing over with.

Beaumont called each one up to testify about my character. He was trying to establish that I was a flight risk or too violent to be let out on bond. Every single one of them said that I was a great guy and non-violent. They wouldn't say a bad word about me. This went on and on. It was probably the most uncomfortable I had ever been, having all these women under the same roof sitting side by side. But I was impressed with Beaumont. How the fuck had he found all those girls? How the fuck had he known they were all associated with me?

"Beaumont, I don't have all day, and none of these witnesses are doing your case any good. Speed it up!"

said the judge, looking over his glasses at the courtroom that now smelled of fifty shades of perfume. It was intoxicating.

Then Franco stood up and went to the front. I hadn't seen Franco in a long time. Maybe a year back, I had gotten a call from April when she was at the club, and she told me that there was a guy there giving her a hard time who wouldn't leave her alone. April was a smart girl and could take care of herself, so it must have been pretty serious for her to call me at home in bed in the middle of the night. I had jumped in my car and gotten over there as quickly as I could. Franco was a big, muscular dude, and he was loud and drunk.

"Hey, what's your name?" I asked.

"Franco," he slurred.

"I'm the owner of the club. Can we step outside for a minute?" I said as I put my hand on his back and led him to the back door. One of the staff or a patron had called the police already.

When we got outside, I asked him what was going on.

"Nothin, nothin."

"Well, April said you were being aggressive and putting your hands on her. She's my girlfriend, and I would appreciate it if you would be respectful of that," I said in a firm, business-like manner.

"Oh! You're the boyfriend." His eyes got wide. They were bloodshot from all the smoke in the club and the alcohol he had consumed.

The cops arrived. Franco had sobered up a bit after being in the fresh air and came to his senses. The police filed a police report, but that had been the end of it.

Franco got up on the stand. He looked fidgety and uncomfortable. They asked him the same questions they'd asked the women.

"I don't have anything against Jimmy," he said, looking like a deer in headlights. "And now, knowing who he is, I would never disrespect his lady."

Beaumont knew he was at the end of the rope if he wanted to keep me in jail until my trial. "Didn't you file a police report against James Keene one night outside his strip club? Tell me about that," Beaumont said in an authoritative voice.

"I was at the club, and I was really digging one of the girls. I was real drunk and guess I was coming on strong. I don't know."

"Did you have an altercation with Mr. Keene?" The irritation showed in Beaumont's voice.

"Well, yeah. We went outside, and he told me to leave her and all the other girls alone. But he was right. I was really drunk. I said I was sorry. He was right."

Franco was dismissed.

"It's getting late, and it's almost lunch," the judge said, "so you'd better find something in your favor, or we're done here, prosecutor."

The final person to take the stand was my previous long-term girlfriend, April.

"How do you know Mr. Keene?"

April was a very soft-spoken woman. "He's my ex-boyfriend."

"How long were you together?" Beaumont asked.

"Around fifteen years, I guess."

"So come on—you can tell me you've seen the famous Jimmy Keene temper. Don't lie to me. You're on the stand."

"No, never. He's never lost his temper with me in all the time I've known him."

"Come on. You're telling me he never came home and got angry about dinner not being on the table or the dishes not being done?" You've never squabbled about anything in fifteen years?" Beaumont had been calm throughout the proceedings, but his voice started to rise.

"No, never."

"Judge, you can clearly see that this woman is terrified of Keene," he suddenly shouted. "She's clearly a victim of domestic abuse and terrified of Mr. Keene and what he'll do to her." Beaumont picked up a book and slammed it on the floor. "Don't lie! You're afraid of Keene. Tell the truth!"

April, in the same soft-spoken voice, looked directly at him. "No, Mr. Prosecutor. I have never *ever* been afraid of Jimmy. But I *am* afraid of you."

With that, the media in the back of the courtroom started taking pictures. There was a loud buzz as all the people in the courtroom chatted among themselves.

The judge watched the proceedings looking unimpressed. "I don't know where you're going with all of this, Beaumont. You're free to step down, ma'am." He let out a big sigh. "Bail set at two million dollars. Dismissed." He was noticeably annoyed by the waste of time the questioning had become.

When everyone had filed out of the courtroom, I saw April sitting alone in a corner. I started toward her.

My lawyer grabbed me. "No, that's not advisable."

"I just want to go make sure she's okay." They allowed me to go and console her.

When she saw me approaching, her big brown eyes filled with tears. She was scared by the whole ordeal and worried about me. I put my arm around her and pulled her close.

"I hope I didn't do anything to hurt you in there, Jimmy."

I laughed to ease her worries. "No, no, April. You were great. You were strong! You stood your ground and really put him in his place."

While I was out on bail, I needed to get my shit together. I hired a team of attorneys to represent me. I also paid them millions to do so. When I sat down with them, they were confident about my chances of avoiding jail time even though the Feds had a ninety-nine-percent conviction rate.

"Your criminal history is clean. They don't have much on you. Based on the charges and the evidence, you should be looking at no more than probation or up to eighteen months in jail."

"Okay, and?"

"And, if you take the deal and plead guilty to the minor charges they've put against you, you'll most likely only get probation."

I did what they suggested at our next court hearing a short while later. I announced my intention to take the plea deal, but Beaumont had more up his sleeve than we realized. We hadn't counted on Beaumont adding superseding federal conspiracy charges.

"Your honor," Beaumont declared to the judge, "the federal government has additional charges for Mr. Keene, namely conspiracy with the intent to deliver. We have federal witness testimony against Mr. Keene supporting this charge, and based on the quantity of drugs these confidential informants said they witnessed in Mr. Keene's possession over a ten-year period, he meets the guidelines for a mandatory minimum sentence of twenty years to life in prison."

As I listened dumbfounded to the words "twenty years to life," phantom flashes popped in my peripheral vision like fireworks, numbing my senses and setting off a steady ringing in my ears as my mind grappled with the shock of what I'd just heard. *Twenty to life? What happened to probation?* As the judge finished the proceedings, my thoughts buzzed. *Confidential informants? Who did they talk into rolling on me?* I trusted my crew, and I ran a careful business.

I discussed the matter with my lawyers immediately. Their confidence had evaporated into grim concern. "Well, it appears they have two informants who will testify against you. That means they have a proffer agreement—a behind-closed-doors deal about what the informants are going to testify to against you and what sort of deal the Feds will give them in exchange. It'll all be settled before they testify. If they've told the prosecutors anything especially incriminating, they might nail you with the mandatory minimum sentence. This could become very serious."

"How serious?"

"One of them has given testimony saying they've seen you in possession of enough cocaine to put you three grams over the necessary limit needed to have a mandatory minimum sentence of twenty years to life. When you reach a mandatory minimum, there's not much we can do. The judge has no say in the matter—it's strictly the prosecutor who decides, and you're required to do the mandatory minimum sentence—no time off for good behavior. It's a bad deal—advocate groups have been trying to fight mandatory minimums for years. If you get into trouble while you're incarcerated, they'll add additional time to your sentence. They can keep doing that for years—for the rest of your life."

"Is there anything we can do?"

"We can demand an evidentiary hearing. The informants would have to appear on the stand to testify and undergo cross-examination about their testimonies. It might help undermine their credibility, so we'll see what we can do." That was all the hope they could leave me with.

This was all sobering news. We didn't know how the charges would shake out, and I didn't have any idea who the informants could be or what the hearing would do to my case. I went on with my daily life, but there was a persistent knot of uncertainty in my stomach. I decided to liquidate my legitimate businesses and put some money in the bank for the expenses coming down the pike.

One day, I was driving back home from my dad's place on my motorcycle. I had my current girlfriend, Tina, with me. I had stopped at a red light when another motorcycle pulled up beside me. I looked over and I saw it was Richie. I hadn't seen him for several weeks since our arrest. He hadn't been staying at the house, but that wasn't unusual now that he had a girlfriend.

He saw me and started crying. Not just a little bit, either—tears streamed down his face. He was trying to speak but appeared to be overcome by his emotion.

"Richie, what's the deal?"

"Jimmy, man." He took a long pause to collect himself. "I'm so sorry, man. They—they made me do this. I didn't want to."

I realized immediately what he was saying, and my stomach dropped—Richie was one of the informants. I was silent for a moment, and I didn't respond. He was too tied up in his own agony to notice. I was floored at how corrupt a system must be to push people into confessing things that broke them up this much. How much had they pressured him and promised to convince him to betray all of the years Richie and I had between us? How terrified had he been to cave to their demands?

I closed my eyes, still averting my gaze. "Man, you're a federal witness. You have to get away from me. If somebody drives by in traffic and sees you sitting here at a light, and you're crying, they're going to go tell the police that I'm threatening you. That makes it automatic—an additional ten years for threatening a federal witness."

Richie choked down a sob. "What do you want me to do?"

I told him to meet me out in the country behind an old, abandoned church we both knew about. We pulled around to the back of the church, and as soon as we got parked, he got off his motorcycle and dropped down on his knees sobbing and begging me for forgiveness. He just kept crying and crying. "What can I do? I'm so sorry. They made me do this."

"What you can do, Richie, is go in there and change your testimony. They've got me for just three grams—barely over the mandatory minimum limit. *Your* testimony is forcing me into a twenty-to-life category."

He sobered up like a drunk, still down on his knees. "I—I can't do that."

"Well, then we have nothing to talk about, man. Our friendship is over. You're nothing but a narc—a rat—a snitch in my book, man. Get away from me." I jumped on my motorcycle where Tina waited, and I left.

While I was out on bail, my brother, Tim, had a baby. Tim named him Timothy James Keene—named after both of us. They called him TJ. In February, when he was about six weeks old, TJ died of SIDS. His mom had left him at daycare on her very first day back to work, and when she'd gone to pick him up, they told her that he was still asleep in his crib. She went to go get him, but he wasn't breathing. He'd spit up while lying face down on his stomach and had died.

Our family was beyond devastated. Tim was heart-broken—inconsolable. We held the funeral sometime in March, and as our group of family and friends grieved and lingered near the end of the wake, Richie showed up. Everybody knew he was the narc by then. I saw him through the crowd but didn't get near him—I didn't want to catch another ten years. But I watched as my brother and Kevin confronted him. "Richie, you asshole, what the hell are you doing showing your face here?"

"I'm so sorry, Tim. I know I messed up big. I know Jimmy didn't deserve me turning on him. But I'm so sorry about your baby boy. I had to come—not coming would have just been another thing I'd done wrong, you know? Please—please—I'm sorry for all of it."

Tim's face was like granite. The crushing weight of grief and betrayal had turned him to stone. He and Kevin advanced on Richie, backing him up the way he'd come in, with determined, deliberate steps.

"If you were sorry, you wouldn't go through with it," Kevin said, sneering at Richie's sniveling. "You would take it all back and admit you felt pressured to say what you did." He spat at Richie's feet. "But you're too worried about your own skin to think about what you're doing to Jimmy—even after all those times he saved your worthless hide. You'd be dead without him. You're pitiful." Their eyes held the threat of violence, and

Richie knew better than to push the issue. He made a hurried exit before they could strike.

I just shook my head. Richie had audacity to show up at my little nephew's wake during the time we were both out on bond. I didn't know if it was good or bad of him to do that. I didn't know *what* to think.

Only a week later, we lost my Aunt Sharon as well. When that news hit me, I thought the disasters would never end. Aunt Sharon was one of the most wonderful, beautiful people I'd ever known—truly a magnificent soul. We'd always been close. She'd been diagnosed out of the blue with stage-four lung cancer, and she was gone in a flash. She hadn't even realized how sick she was before it was far too late. She died at forty-nine and left me with another hole in my heart from the blast.

My life at that point felt like a dark, muddy battle-field, and I had artillery shells raining down all around me as I dragged through with my face flat in the filth. I didn't know when the next one would hit or how much more wreckage it would cause, and my trial was less than a month away. I didn't know what could possibly happen next to make things worse, but I would soon find out. The war was far from over, and I had a long way left to crawl.

CHAPTER 10

HEARSAY AND OTHER BULLSHIT

My mind was reeling on the day of the evidentiary hearing. I couldn't believe I was in this situation. My lawyers said the hearing would call the Feds' bluff. I knew Richie was a rat—I was still angry and hurt over that. But I had no clue who the other confidential informant could be.

As they escorted me into the courtroom and to the defendant's seat, I saw my family sitting near the middle of the room. Dad did not look as tall and proud as I loved seeing him. Tim, who was still grappling with the loss of his baby boy, looked ready to drop from the sorrow. My mom, sister, and half-sister sat on the row behind. I saw Mom's tear-filled eyes follow me as I walked by.

I sat down next to my lawyers, and they gave me an encouraging smile. But behind their eyes, I glimpsed a flash of doubt that froze my core. What would happen if they sent me away for twenty years? My life would be ruined. All that hard life-or-death work to reach the top of the mountain, get ten million in the bank, and walk away never to deal with drugs again had been flushed away. I had been close—so close—but now nothing would ever be the same. Twenty years in prison would change a man. Perhaps this was just another foreboding piece of what was bound to be my ill-fated destiny. No matter how hard I tried to force my fortunes into a better trajectory, the gutters I had been raised in just pulled me right back into the darkness.

We were asked to stand as the judge entered. *Let the circus begin*, I thought wryly.

Beaumont called upon his first witness to testify against me. I cast what I hoped would look like a casual glance behind me as the witness approached. I felt a knife slice through my heart—it was Brandy. I couldn't believe it. *It must be a mistake.* Brandy and I had grown up together. We had known each other just as long as anyone else in my life. We'd dated for years! After we broke up, she'd moved on to an abusive husband and then to another one. She'd had no real means of supporting her two children from either marriage, so I'd paid her to clean my house, hired her to work at the club as a cleaner, and did whatever else I could to help her out. Never in a million years had I thought that kindness and all those years together would be thrown aside and that she would stab me deep in the back.

My brain raced. I didn't hear the first half of what Brandy said as I started connecting the dots in my mind—Brandy had seen my saferoom. That was how the Feds had found it so quickly.

I hadn't really thought too much about it at the time, but Richie had also been busted after buying product from Brandy. She must have set Richie up for that bust in order to get to me. Brandy's preferred drug dealers were the gang members on the South Side. I considered all of the people that were in the drunk tank with Richie and me when we were rounded up and indicted—now it all made sense. She must have gotten busted and set them up, too. Law enforcement had used a simple tactic: bust a drug user and make her turn on her small-time dealer. Bust the dealer and get to the next bigger fish. It was all about using the right bait for the next trophy up the line. Why hadn't she come to me to ask for help? *Why would she do this?*

As I refocused on the scene before me, I heard my lawyer questioning Brandy.

"What time of year did this happen, Miss Morris?"

Brandy kept looking at me, her eyes wide and her hands pulling at her dress. She was nervous and not a very good liar.

"I don't recall."

"Okay, so you met him at the fairgrounds, but you don't remember what time of the year it was. Was it cold? Hot?" my lawyer went on.

"I don't recall."

"You don't remember the time of year or what the weather was like? Do you remember the time of day this transaction happened?"

"I don't recall."

"Do you remember what Mr. Keene was driving when he met you?"

"I don't recall."

"Do you remember the dialogue you and Mr. Keene shared when you met him?"

"I don't recall."

"Do you remember what Mr. Keene was wearing when you say you met him?"

"I don't recall."

"Miss Morris! You want me to believe that you can't remember the time of the year, the weather, the time of day, or any other details, but you *do* remember the exact amount of cocaine you purchased from the defendant? Do you remember how much you paid for the bag you bought?"

"I don't recall."

This went on and on. *How can this shit even be used as legal valid evidence?* I wondered. When I finally got the court transcriptions afterward, the lawyers had asked Brandy hundreds of questions, and she'd answered them all the same way, the same word "I don't recall".

Brandy returned to her seat at the conclusion of the questions looking fearful, small, and drained of energy. But the time she spent in court that day wasn't the full price Brandy paid for testifying against me and all of the others she'd acted as an informant against. Her actions had made a lot of people angry, put a lot of people in prison, and hurt a lot of drug operations. Someone else got wind of who the main snitch in the indictment was, and that someone tracked Brandy down. One day years after the dust from operation snowplow had settled, Brandy was walking down a street when someone put a gun to her head and pulled the trigger.

When I heard, I was even more heartbroken than I had been before. Had it all really been worth her life? When the feds pressured her into lying about drug deals, turning on a lifelong friend, and then setting up more deals to catch buyers, they'd gambled with her life, and she'd been the one to pay the consequences—not them.

And Brandy *had* been lying. I had never sold anyone product directly since my whole enterprise began. I had never met her at the fairground or anywhere else she had claimed to buy drugs directly from me.

After Brandy's testimony in the courtroom, I realized something truly sobering: *I may not be able to beat this.* This was the legal system. The skills I'd honed while growing up had not prepared me for this. I couldn't fight my way out, beat someone up, or even talk my way out of it. My gut twisted, and my heart filled with despair.

Next to take the stand was Richie. As he walked past me, he looked at me with pain in his eyes. His eyes scanned the room like a scared rabbit as he took his seat. He pulled at his necktie as if to loosen a noose around his neck.

"Mr. O'Reilly, how do you know Mr. Keene?"

"We grew up together," Richie said, looking at me. I stared back with a stony expression.

"When you met Mr. Keene on the night of October 10, 1992, how much cocaine did you buy?"

Richie glanced at me again and then back at the prosecutor. "I don't know. Maybe a dime bag." He pulled at his collar again.

This wasn't the large amount Richie had previously claimed, and I could see Beaumont's subtle reaction to this undesirable change of plan. I felt the ice in my stomach warm ever so slightly—Richie had given in, at least partially. He was changing his testimony. Beaumont marched resolutely up to the stand, and his voice grew louder. "Are you sure, Mr. O'Reilly? You're under oath."

"It was a long time ago. Yeah, I think so." Richie pulled his necktie back and forth.

"Was the bag this big?" Beaumont asked, showing the size of his palm.

"No, no. It was much smaller." Richie's gaze met mine again.

Beaumont raised his voice again. "I repeat, you are under oath. Look at my palm—was it this big?"

The testimony went on for a long time. And Richie didn't budge. Because he had changed the product amount from his previous statement, the charges against me no longer met the mandatory minimum for twenty years to life, and the Feds were forced to lower the sentence to ten years to life.

Years later, after I'd punched my ticket out of prison, I heard from Richie again. He was still kicking around, but his life was still a mess. When he found out that my story was becoming popular, he called me.

"Hey Jimmy, how're you doing?"

"I'm fine, Richie. What's up?"

"I saw you on *Dateline*. That was pretty cool, huh?"

"Yeah, I guess so." There was a long pause.

"What do you want, Richie?"

"I was just wondering if you could help me out, man. You know that whole ordeal back then—you know I'm sorry. It really messed up my life. I'm really struggling."

I let out a hard sigh. I guessed some things never really changed. "Goodbye, Richie."

When the judge handed down my sentence, I couldn't feel my body. I felt someone reach under my arm and try to pull me to my feet. In the background, I could hear my mother crying hysterically. I could hear my father speaking to my brother in an angry voice about injustice. And as I pondered what lay in my immediate future, I couldn't believe that my life had come to this when twelve months ago—hell, six months ago—I was on top of the world with everything a man could ask for. I had nearly decided to be done with the drug business forever. As the deputies walked me out of the courtroom, I looked over at my dejected, melancholy family and friends. Each one of them had tears in his or her eyes.

When I settled in for the night in my cell, it was hard to imagine what the next ten years would look like or to think of the things I would miss. I had hit rock bottom, and there was no way out other than doing the time handed down to me.

The next morning, they prepared to move me over to the MCC facility. This was an interesting place. It sat in the middle of Chicago towering over many of the buildings there. If you flew over it, you would see a basketball court and a workout area on the roof covered in a cage of wire. Every floor was filled with angry people and ugly conflict. It was a halfway house of sorts. People like me went there to wait for their assignments to more permanent facilities—to the prisons they would call home while serving their sentences. Other inmates were there waiting to go on trial, and everyone was pissed off.

Since it was a holding facility, they didn't have all the policies and procedures needed to prevent horrible things from happening between prisoners. And honestly, I don't think they really gave a shit. They didn't group you by the seriousness of your crime, ethnic group, or anything else that seemed logical. There were extremely violent inmates, sex offenders, murderers, and people charged with assault piled in with white-collar crime offenders and prisoners with nonviolent drug charges. One wrong move could mean the end of your life if you pissed the wrong person off. The gangster John Gotti said the worst hell he ever experienced was the MCC in New York. In my opinion, the MCC in Chicago was even worse.

My survival instincts went on high alert in that place. They told me it would take weeks for my papers to come through and for the transfer to happen. The main area was a large room where people could watch TV in a corner. There were microwaves on another wall for heating up food items. But the rest of the rooms were rows and rows of bunk beds. People would claim one, and that was their only real "personal" space.

The second day I was there, I got a new bunkmate. His name was Derek. If I'd ever seen a surfer dude, this cat was definitely one. He had long hair bleached blonde from the sun, a wiry muscular build, and a big, white-toothed smile reflecting off his tanned skin. His preferred activities were surfing all day and smoking weed at beach parties all night—an eat-pray-love type of guy.

We had spoken some about where we were from, our families, and other minor topics. He said he was from California. They had sentenced him to seventy years to life for a marijuana conspiracy. I didn't know why they had incarcerated him so far away from California, but he definitely stuck out like a sore thumb in Chicago. I learned later that if someone wouldn't cooperate, sometimes the Feds would send them to a holding facility across the country as punishment.

At night, it was like sleeping in the jungle. If anything was going to go down, this was when it would happen. The guards only came by every so often to patrol the room and make sure everyone was in a bed. I awoke one night to scuffling sounds above me, and when I opened my eyes, I saw at least twelve men around our bunk. They were pulling Derek off the bunk. They had stuffed a towel in his mouth, and they carried him off into the darkness. I knew nothing good was going to come from this, but I also knew I couldn't do anything to help without getting myself targeted or killed.

There were a few people awake that I saw rolling in the other direction to show they were not going to alert the guards or make themselves targets as well. All night, we could hear Derek screaming and whimpering. Each time the guards came by, they would put him in an empty bunk and probably threaten his life if he uttered a noise. This went on all night long.

In the morning, Derek limped over to his old bunk, and I hardly recognized him. His hair had been pulled up into sloppy pigtails, and his face was swollen, bruised, and bloody. On top of his injuries, his face had been painted with purple Kool-Aid staining his eyelids and red smeared on his cheeks and lips. Prison make-up. I noticed twelve to fifteen large and muscular Black men watching to see if Derek said anything to me or to anyone else. He looked at me with tears in his eyes, collected his belongings, and went to another bunk.

I never knew what happened to Derek after that. The guards came to get him later that day, either to place him somewhere else or move him to his next destination. The reality of my future was really sinking in.

Not all the people I associated with in the MCC were rough people. Some of them were smart and savvy about surviving and protecting themselves in our volatile and violent environment. Others were educated or successful men who had simply made decisions that came back to bite them. A few of them taught me things I needed in order to keep my sanity and my life intact.

Malcolm Shady was a Black, middle-class computer hacker genius. He was also my bunkmate. He'd been convicted of identity theft and hacking into government mainframe computers and causing sabotage. He was always trying to pass on his technical skill and knowledge to whomever would listen:

"Hey, Jimmy, you want to know how to get someone's bank account number with an email? It's easy. Let me tell you."

Shady wasn't a physically formidable guy—more the typical nerd, really—and he seemed eager to bolster his reputation by relating his misdeeds. Even in prison, where most inmates haven't done much to deserve admiration by society's standards, people crave the respect of those around them.

One inmate named Charles Green was instrumental in forming the El Rukn group in South Side Chicago. El Rukn was the group that had formerly been known as the Blackstone Rangers, and they were one of the most powerful and notorious street gangs in Chicago.

"Mr. Green," as Green's Black supporters in the MCC called him, was not what a person might expect had they known his background. He was a middle-aged Black man, and although he had legions of El Rukn gang members ready to defend him at any moment, he didn't seem to relish violence. I'll never forget the day I first spoke to him. He was standing behind me in line at the sink. It had been a stressful first week, and the strain of prison life was building inside me like a pressure cooker. I was brushing my teeth and absorbed in my problems. As I straightened to leave, I heard a voice behind me say, "Hey, boy. Why don't you rinse out that sink when you're done."

I snapped and wheeled on the man behind me. "Don't you tell me what to do! If it's so important to you, do it yourself!" I yelled in his face.

Faster than I could blink, a mob of Black prisoners rushed to Green's defense. They surrounded the two of us like a pack of angry wolves eager to spring into action. I was poised and eager to take on the whole group—it would have felt good to bust some faces in that hellish place and release some of my frustration, but then I looked at Green. His placid, calming expression snuffed out my flame of anger.

"Take it easy, kid," he told me, calling off his protectors with a lift of his hand. The gesture looked casual, but I couldn't help but feel impressed at how the wave of tension in the room was diffused with such a small motion. Green made eye contact with me and held his hand out toward the open general area. I gritted my teeth and walked the way he'd directed, knowing that he intended to follow me there.

"No, not this way. Follow me," he said as he veered off in a different direction and came to a door. The guard opened the door.

We walked into the next room, which was the same size as the one I was in, but the setup was much different. Instead of the bunks being bunched in the middle of the room, there were six to eight bunks with partitions on two sides to give the occupants a little more privacy.

"Hey, I didn't know this was even here. It must be nice to have some privacy."

"This is for us guys who have been here for a while. Flight risks who didn't make bail. Guys they haven't figured out where to put yet. Or some of us that have favors with the guards."

When we entered, he directed me to sit on a bunk with yet another silent motion.

"If you want to survive in here, you're going to have to manage that hot head of yours."

I was quiet for a moment. My pulse still beat in my ears from the barely avoided violence. He waited until I answered, "Feels more like it's the only thing keeping me alive."

"I see why you might think that. But it's not true." He locked his gaze with mine, his voice low and deliberate. "Look around you, kid. You're tough. I saw you stare down that whole hoard of men ready to tear you apart. You would have lasted longer than most men in that situation, sure. But tough will only get you so far in here. Winning fights in this place won't win you much of anything. It won't win you any respect."

I didn't answer. The bad energy in this place made me antsy as hell. Green calmly surveyed my silent tension and continued.

"You push enough buttons and make enough enemies with that short fuse of yours, and most of the mad dogs in this fine establishment won't think twice about killing you at the earliest opportunity. They *will* either kill you or scar you for life. If you manage to stay alive, you'll still have big problems. In here, the guards are in charge. Blowing your stack about every little thing will put you on their bad side in a serious way, and there's no fighting fair with the guards. They got advantages you don't. They can hold every detail of your life over your head. They'll put you in solitary. And they can put a beating on even the toughest of the tough." He sighed, finally breaking eye contact to survey the hallway with cool calm. "Trust me—you don't want that."

His words washed over my harried mind and slowly seeped into my core. I knew he was right. I'd navigated enough sticky situations to see that the pressure in this place was messing with my usual ability to read the room and respond strategically. I didn't know why a powerful man like Mr. Green with the sort of past he'd had would bother to help me keep my head above water. He certainly didn't have to. I didn't know what was in it for him, but I was grateful.

Finally, I nodded my thanks to him. He returned the nod and strolled back out of my cell without another word. After that, Green and I became pretty friendly, despite him being a man with four life sentences to his name.

Green pulled some strings and invited me to move to the more private bunk room into a cubical bed of my own. I was relieved to leave my old bunk behind. My new bunkmate was the reverse of Green's paradoxical persona.

"Keene, this is Robinson. Robinson, Keene." Robinson was a light-skinned Black man with an upright posture and an educated air about him. Robinson nodded to me, and I nodded back. Being a man with influence myself, I could see that this man was accustomed to being in charge and had a lofty opinion of himself. But he was also an agreeable enough neighbor.

Noah Robinson Jr. had been involved with El Rukn as well and had gone to trial as a codefendant with Green because he'd used El Rukn's powerful presence in the city to support his under-the-table business dealings and South Side drug enterprise. He'd also hired them to carry out more than one hit, though the final attempt hadn't been successful. Robinson had been rich and privileged before diving into Chicago's underworld dealings.

On the outside, Robinson didn't seem like the type of guy to get tangled in all of that. Everything about him signified that he was a reputable, successful businessman. His half-brother was the Reverend Jesse Jackson. Robinson had an MBA and a refined personality and manner that would have fit right in with the rich, elite politicians of Chicago.

How Robinson ended up in MCC didn't add up to me at first. I'd put everything into building my drug business, but if I hadn't been raised in the poverty and crime that I had been, I didn't think I would have followed the same path that had eventually brought me here. Robinson, on the other hand, seemed to have given away his security, education, and respectability in exchange for a dangerous, volatile lifestyle. I decided that even men who seem to have everything want more, and they want to get it as fast and as easily as possible. Sometimes they're willing to do anything for it. It was common knowledge in my former line of business that the rich and powerful usually had surprising secrets. Robinson's had landed him with a life sentence.

CHAPTER 11

A TICKET TO MILAN

When the Feds decided where your permanent home within the prison system was going to be, they gathered you up without any warning or notice about your final destination. You might end up at any federal prison in the country. They'd group you with the rest of the transferring inmates, put you in handcuffs, and shackle your feet. If you were transferring any significant distance, they transported you by plane. Airports used specific airplanes for "Con Air." It was just like the movie with Nicholas Cage. As we got off the van and herded to the airplane, hundreds of guards surrounded the vans and the plane, all guns pointed and ready to fire if needed. We were all chained together and loaded into the back of a cargo plane outfitted with long bench seats so that we could sit down still chained to the inmates on either side. Con Air sucked. It was an uncomfortable flying prison of the friendly skies.

The airplanes didn't have numbers on them. They did this so nobody could find which plane held a certain inmate and try to sabotage the plane to kill them or force it down to free them. Even though it was a quick trip from the Chicago airport to Detroit, where I ultimately would land, that was not how Con-Air worked. The routes the Feds used to get us all where we were going were circuitous and lengthy—some of the worst, time-wasting layovers you can imagine. They called these transports "diesel therapy." These cargo planes were not like the normal commercial planes people took. They smelled strongly of fuel. And it could take weeks or even months to get to your final stop.

After our initial takeoff, we landed in Oklahoma, which was the nicest stop of all the temporary depots I visited. We stayed there for over a week, and then they hauled us off on another identical plane to another airport, this time in Indiana, then to New York, and then Missouri. After several weeks of this, I landed in Michigan and learned my new home would be the Federal Correctional Institute in Milan—another hell hole thinly veiled behind a flowery title.

When we finally arrived at FCI Milan, they processed us in, and we got our cell assignments. At first, I was assigned to B block, a barracks-style block that allowed cigarette smoking. I immediately went to the doctor and showed him my medical form stating that I was allergic to cigarette smoke, and I was then transferred to H block, a nonsmoking cell block. I was surprised to find I was on the top tier of cells and on the short wall. The short wall had only two cells, as opposed to the long wall which had thirty to forty. This meant there were fewer people coming along the corridor to pass by my cell and wake me up, and the location was halfway quiet. Not only that, but I was alone. In prison, you learn to appreciate the smallest of luxuries. I felt I had hit the jackpot.

My new neighbor in the adjacent cell saw me come in. He stepped up to the bars to talk to me.

"Hey, welcome to the penthouse! I'm Geoff. What's your name, man?"

"Yeah, this is pretty sweet! I'm Jimmy."

"Stick with me, Jimmy. This place isn't so bad. I've been here for a long time. I'll show you the ropes. Trust me, I've been in a lot worse. Do you work out?"

"Fuck, yeah. It's a must," I said, looking down at my arms. They hadn't seen a proper workout since I'd been indicted.

"They have some decent space for that. The food will about kill ya, though, and there is more rust than water coming outta the pipes, but overall—for prison—I guess it's okay."

They released us about thirty minutes later for the daily routine of chow, and I followed Geoff to the cafeteria. When I got to the front of the line, my heart sank. There wasn't a fresh fruit or vegetable in sight. The pancakes I stacked on my tray were cold and rubbery.

Man, I'll never survive ten years of this shit in my body. All these years of keeping myself in shape and eating healthy, for what? How do they expect someone to live like this? And everyone else is just eating this slop. Shit in, shit out.

A few weeks passed, and I could feel my body revolting against the shit food and water. One day as a guard came by, I whistled to get his attention.

"Hey, man, sorry to bother you. Is there someone I can speak to? This water is causing me some real issues," I said. I knew complaining was a risk. If you complain to the wrong guard, they can really make your life hell.

"You're new here, right?" The guard said.

"Yeah. I'm Keene.

The guard pulled my file out of the file box on my door. "Oh man, how did a guy like you end up here?" He was grinning from ear to ear.

I watched him for a second, wondering if he was being sarcastic or malicious with that comment, but the expression in his eyes looked genuine.

"No problem, man. I'll set you up with the good doctor. The other one is a real asshole. He wakes up on the wrong side of the bed every day. He won't help."

"Thanks, man! I really appreciate that. What's your name?" I couldn't believe how nice this guy was. It was so refreshing.

"Call me Surf. No Problem. Let me know if you need anything. I'll help ya out if I can."

A week later, I was called down to the medical building. The doctor was a middle-aged woman with dark hair and glasses. The only thing about her that didn't look like it belonged on a librarian was the stethoscope around her neck and the medical smock. She was very polite and listened to me. She reviewed my file from my regular doctor. He had written up a detailed medical report to the prison doctors letting them know that his lifelong patient had medical conditions that warranted clean water and food. My pre-prison doctor was a lifelong friend and didn't think I should have been sent to prison on a draconian hearsay conspiracy case. He wanted to help me in any way he could. His medical report won me a lot of special privileges. Prison doctors cannot override your long-term doctor's demands.

Due to my file, the doctor in Milan didn't really test much before she diagnosed me with an allergic reaction to the water and ordered that I be always provided with bottled water. Now I could finally feel like I wasn't poisoning myself with every drink of water I took.

Water quality was a big problem in those old prison systems, sometimes causing serious health problems including Legionnaires' disease, which is a serious form of pneumonia. Thanks to my allergic reaction, I was also no longer required to work in the factory and didn't have to breathe in that crap air. Next, I decided to find a way to stop eating that shitty processed food. My entrepreneurial instincts sparked and roared to life like the engine of one of the fancy cars I'd left back home—I had a problem I needed to solve, and I would solve it one way or another.

A few days later, Surf came by my cell with three gallons of bottled water from the dispenser in the staff room. "Special delivery, Keene!" He unlocked my door and let himself in.

"Hey, thanks for getting me to that doctor. She really hooked me up!" I said, helping him make room for the new gallon jugs.

"No shit, man! I've been here a long time, and I've never heard of anyone being allowed bottled water! You're turning into a real VIP around here.

Every night, Geoff and I would walk for hours around the track in the exercise facility until they would close down the yard at night. We got really close in a short period of time. He reminded me of my crew on the outside, and that brotherhood bond was something I really missed.

"Hey, Geoff, I have an idea. I know you're in tight with the kitchen crew. I think we can set up our own racket here."

"Yeah, yeah, I know those brothers down there. But they're stingy with any of their food. They don't just give it away. They want small fortunes for even a sniff of an orange peel."

We both laughed. "I think I can get something they'd be willing to give away an orange for," I said.

Over the next couple of weeks, I had friends and family bring in porn magazines every time they visited, and thanks to Surf, I would actually receive them. I had them all stacked up under my mattress and anywhere else I could hide one. Geoff spread the word through our compound that we were open for business, and soon enough I had a line outside my cell.

"Hey, Jimmy," said Jamal, who was the head of the kitchen staff. "I'm looking for a date with Miss April in the new issue of *Swank* for the whole weekend."

"Hey, Jamal. Wow—Miss April from *Swank*. She's a hot one. A whole weekend? That beauty is gonna cost you a lot. What's that worth to ya?" I said as I pulled that issue out from under the mattress, opened up the centerfold, and casually held it up so Jamal could glimpse his prize.

"Man, Jimmy," Jamal said, fidgeting with his eyes fixed on the magazine. I could almost hear him drooling. "I'll give you two watermelons and two whole turkey breasts—you know, the kind you slice for sandwiches—in exchange for the weekend."

I let out an exasperated breath. "Come on. You can do better than that. Add two loaves of whole wheat bread, a bag of apples, and a bunch of bananas, and you have a deal."

"Fo' sure! Anything you want for that Miss April, Jimmy!"

Not only was I hustling porn magazines for food, other favors, or money, but Geoff and I were also selling decent food back to the prisoners for a profit. For prison life, it was a pretty cushy arrangement.

When I found out there were punching bags in the workout room on a lower level, I was excited. I had been taught by my dad and in martial arts how to punch and kick. It was something I'd excelled at since grade school. I had six bags set up in the barn at our home on Skyline, and I would practice diligently every day.

One night, I headed to the stairs that would take me down there, and another prisoner yelled over, "Hey, where are you going?"

"To go check out the punching bags."

"No, man, you can't go down there. Whites aren't allowed down there." He walked closer.

"Well, I'm going." The guy looked at me like I'd just signed my own death sentence.

As I exited the stairway, I saw my goal—the punching bag. Nobody was on it, so I decided to give it a few rounds before going back up. Pretty soon, a little Black man strolled up to me and watched my form.

"Man, you're a great boxer, and your kicks are phenomenal—the best I ever seen. Where'd you learn all that? Who was your trainer?" he asked.

"My dad trained me, and I trained in martial arts and wrestling. I'm more like a UFC guy," I said, not losing a beat on the bag.

"Those kicks are fire, and you got really great boxing skills! Call me Senior," he said as he got on the other side of the bag. "Would you mind if I give you some pointers?"

He started showing me techniques. I enjoyed having him teach me. When I got back upstairs for the night and told Geoff about it, he was amazed.

"You know who he is, right?" Geoff said through the bars of his cell.

"He told me to call him Senior, I think," I said, recalling my earlier conversation.

"Yeah, that's Floyd Mayweather Sr. He got hit with a Fed drug minimum, too."

"No shit! Well, that's cool. He was teaching me some great techniques."

Every day the old guy would meet me down there, and he would train me. Those training sessions were the most positive and joyous memories of my whole prison nightmare.

One day we took a break, and I went into the bathroom that was just around the corner. The bathroom was situated in a blind spot away from the guards' constant attention. As I stood at a urinal doing my thing, another guy with a long ponytail came out of a stall and went to use the urinal a couple of spots down from me. Suddenly, ten massive men came into the bathroom all at once and approached the guy.

When the guy looked up and saw the men behind him, he tried to turn, but they were on him like a mongoose on a cobra. They all carried handmade knives called shanks. They had a brief argument about being ripped off on a drug deal, and before I could react, the ponytailed guy had been stabbed at least a dozen times without a pause. The guy put up a pretty good fight, but he was woefully outmatched. I knew he wouldn't get out of there alive.

I edged backward to the wall and slid toward the door. The main guy looked up from the fight and spotted me. We locked eyes for a beat, his shank glistening with blood, and I held my hand up silently and pointed at the door. I waited, as still as ice, as the guy internally decided whether or not I was next. Finally, with a nod toward the door, he gave me permission to leave, and I kept going as the fight raged on.

I returned to the corner where Senior and the bag waited. He was working the bag over with his easy, powerful skill. Then he saw me approaching and stopped.

"Man, Jimmy, you look like you just seen a ghost! You all right?"

Before I could reply, the alarms started blaring. We got down on the floor with our hands above our heads. We'd had that position drilled into us by the guards. When the alarms sounded, we had to assume that position and stay that way submissively, so the guards knew we weren't causing trouble. It was the best way to make sure we didn't get drawn into something we weren't a part of and didn't get injured or killed.

When I raised my head, Senior was looking at me with sadness in his eyes. About a minute later, guards came around the corner with a body on a stretcher covered in a blood-stained sheet. My life flashed before my eyes.

What the fuck am I thinking? I had gotten into a very comfortable routine—I had surrounded myself with people I felt I could trust. But it was all a facade. At any given time, that could be me on that stretcher or I could be forced to defend myself and put someone else on a stretcher. If that ringleader in the bathroom hadn't let me leave, I could have taken down several of the guys in there, but not before I had a handful of new holes in my body. If just one had hit a vital organ, I would have been gone.

That train of thought shook the very ground I was on for months. So many times, the alarms would go off, and I would look over the tier, and there were the guards going into a cell to pull a body out on a stretcher. I saw the results of suicide attempts, successful suicides, murders, rapes, heart attacks, grisly injuries, and violent deaths. This was the ugly side of life in prison, and no matter how cozy a person got, it was right there ready to slap him in the face if he ever tried to forget about it.

The next week, I was still pretty shaken from the bathroom incident when Surf came into my cell. "How you doin', Jimmy?"

"I'm good, Surf. How're the kids?"

"Freakin' weeds, man! The baby started to walk this weekend. So, listen—we have more inmates coming in this week. We have to give you a cellmate. There are a few from Chicago. Maybe I can get one of them to come in here with you."

"Well, that sucks. It's all good. Thanks for the heads up, man. Just bring someone in who's cool."

The next day, in walked Frank Calabrese Sr. Frank and I knew each other in Chicago. He was in the same mob family I did business with. But Frank was their hitman. He was a vicious killer. This was a man no one wanted on their bad side.

"Jimmy!" He came over and grabbed me by both shoulders and kissed each cheek. "My God, you look good. What are they feeding you in here?"

I was relieved that my cellmate was someone I knew back in Chicago. Frank had mellowed out over the years, and he was really good to me. But once in a while, I would see a glimmer of the old Frank, and that could turn a person's blood to ice. He joined Geoff and me every night as we walked around and around the prison yard and talked. Sometimes we remained silent, lost in our own thoughts. But none of us ever wanted to be idle, so we were always moving.

Frank had an army on the outside and on the inside of Milan. His men followed him everywhere he went. Sometimes it was unnerving, and when he saw that it bothered me, he would give them a nod, and they'd take up positions somewhere nearby to sit and watch their boss—ready to jump into action if needed.

About a month after Frank arrived, I saw Frank's son come in—Frank Jr. Frank Jr. and I had been good friends back in Chicago. We used to hang out in the clubs, and he would always attend my brownstone parties. I didn't want to hurt Frank Sr.'s feelings, so I asked Surf if he could swap their cells. Surf made the switch the next day, and nobody knew I was behind it. They were always changing people around when it pleased the guards.

With Frank Jr. added to our number, we were a small, tight pack. We would walk for hours every night. Frank Jr. seemed to get along well enough with his dad. I never would have guessed there was any serious trouble between them. Sometimes they would get into arguments about the mafia life and throw blame back and forth, and I would play referee and get them both to chill out.

The rest of us weren't aware, but the whole time he spent in Milan, Frank Jr. was wearing a wire in a portable Walkman to collect further evidence against his father for the Feds. A while later, Frank Sr. and Frank Jr. were all over the news. Just like everyone else in America—and especially in Chicago—I watched the whole Operation Family Secrets saga play out over the years that followed. The operation was responsible for bringing the Chicago mob down to its knees, and the ensuing investigation gave the Feds an unprecedented amount of information on the Chicago Mafia and their criminal activities. Frank and Frank Jr. were right in the middle of it.

Frank Jr. had been convicted on drug charges and started the whole operation in 1998 by contacting the Feds and offering to secretly collect incriminating information for them on his father. He told them his father was a dangerous man who should be kept in prison for the rest of his life. Frank Jr. said he'd be willing to do whatever was required to keep his father behind bars. Frank Jr. wanted out of the mafia life and out of his father's control. He decided that cooperating with the Feds was his only way to freedom.

Frank Sr. claimed to me later that the whole thing had been arranged by himself and his son in order to get Frank Jr. released from prison. Frank Sr. said he knew he was stuck there and that he'd told Frank Jr. what to say and what to do in order to give the Feds the information they wanted and earn his freedom. I wasn't sure which story was true, but I never saw anything to indicate that they had a terrible relationship, even though that's what Frank Jr. later claimed to the Feds and to the press.

Thank God Frank Jr. and I never talked about the good old times together in there. I didn't need the Feds breathing down my neck again. Frank Jr. never gave any indication about the secret purpose that had brought him there or his deal with the Feds.

Eventually, the information Frank Jr. supplied led to a trial in 2007 that included five defendants from the Chicago Outfit and brought in more than a hundred witnesses to give evidence on eighteen previously unsolved murders that dated as far back as 1970. All five defendants were declared guilty, and Frank Sr. spent the rest of his life in prison until he died at seventy-five. Frank Jr. wrote a book about the whole thing in 2012 and later moved to Arizona, where he continued to speak publicly about his time with the Chicago Outfit despite the potential danger to his life.

It wasn't too long after Frank Jr. arrived that Beaumont requested I be sent back to Chicago for that infamous meeting concerning a secret mission of my own for the Feds. At the time I didn't know anything. I had to say I was going back to Chicago to work on my appeals. When Beaumont first offered me the deal to go to the Medical Center for Federal Prisoners in Springfield, I couldn't tell anyone. I did break the rules and talk to my dad about it, and he was adamant that I refuse the deal. I had a decent life in Milan. It was still dangerous, but I had learned how to keep myself safe and how to procure a few comforts. I had friendships to pass the time.

Springfield wouldn't be just another Milan—it was a dangerous maximum-security facility full of unbalanced, unpredictable psychopathic prisoners, and if they discovered why I was there, I would be in serious trouble. I agreed with my dad and refused Beaumont's offer. That is, until I got a visit from my sister Terri. Terri kept in touch throughout my time in prison and was a great support to me. But this visit was more serious than a routine social call.

When she walked into the visiting area, the tense, haggard expression on her face told me something was wrong. She didn't bother with pleasantries. "Jimmy, I have really bad news. Dad had a stroke."

I felt like someone had slammed me in the gut with the end of a two-by-four out of nowhere. Of all the bad news I'd received in the recent past, this was not something I had ever expected. I finally spoke. "How bad is it? Is he alive?"

"He's still hanging in there, but it's bad, Jimmy. He's not doing well." She shared the brief details and what little she knew. She didn't have much to offer by way of comfort—nothing could fix news like this. But I thanked her for her visit, and she left promising to update me all she could over the phone.

I was in a panic. I couldn't see him, and I didn't know what was going on. The days crept by filled with anxiety and torturous silence. The only time I could speak with my family between visits was the allotted telephone time. I prayed each time they answered that they wouldn't tell me it was too late to ever see my dad again. But Dad was a fighter.

The next visiting day, Tim rolled Dad into the room in a wheelchair. One side of Dad's face was droopy. Seeing him like that was hard to swallow. He looked like a shell of the strong man I'd known all of my life. I knew right then that if I had to stay in Milan for ten years, he would likely be gone long before I got out. And it was at that moment I decided I would do whatever it took to get that deal. Nothing would stand in my way. I was heading into the depths of hell—into the belly of the beast—but I wanted out. I wanted my life back before Dad could never be a part of it again.

CHAPTER 12

FIRST CLASS TO SPRINGFIELD

I was filled with apprehension when the time came to transfer to Springfield. I didn't know much about the MCFP in Springfield specifically, but I knew that maximum-security prisons took the dangers and restrictions of prison life to an even higher level and housed some of the country's worst. The FBI informed me of my new backstory: I was charged with trafficking firearms across state lines. This more serious charge would allow me to be housed in a maximum-security facility without raising suspicion.

This new undercover mission wasn't just risky because of where I was going and how dangerous it would be. I had lost my life of luxury when I'd been arrested, but then I had built a fairly tolerable existence at Milan. Aside from freedom, I had what I needed there to get by, and it was a new leap of faith to leave what little I did have behind all over again. I was starting over—but not at a place I intended to stay.

Failure at Springfield was not an option. If I ended up shipped back to Milan, I would lose every advantage I had secured. I knew what little comfort I had made for myself in Milan would be snatched up by other inmates as soon as I left, and I didn't think they would just give it back.

The other possibility that came with failure was that I would end up stuck in Springfield for my entire sentence, or even that I would have to protect myself and earn additional time. That was an even more horrific thought. My life was suspended in limbo between a lot of bad options, and I had a host of seemingly impossible battles to fight and information to acquire in frighteningly hostile territory before any better options would present themselves. I didn't know how I was going to do what I needed to, but at least I was already accustomed to meeting insurmountable odds head on.

I've related the events that occurred in Springfield with Larry Hall before, and I'll retell some of it here. Beaumont gave me a large file on Hall to read and study, but the only time I could really do that in private was late at night. I memorized everything about the guy, but Beaumont didn't give me details about the actual murders.

I was told not to approach Hall before I'd been in Springfield for six months. I was supposed to let him get accustomed to seeing me around before I even tried to speak to him. The FBI gave me a training manual for how to obtain information under the radar. I was supposed to eavesdrop, get to know Hall and his serial-killer friends, and wait around until they let valuable information slip out. I didn't think that was the right approach, and some of the FBI agents I worked with to prepare were upset if I talked about handling it differently.

Once, they asked me what I planned to do. I answered, "I never plan anything." Their boss believed I had a better skillset to get the job done than an agent, so I figured I shouldn't try to change who I was or how I approached things. I listened to the FBI agents' advice, but I knew that I would have to handle this daring mission my way and use the skills I had developed in the life-or-death situations I'd encountered previously.

The FBI introduced me to an attractive blonde agent who would come in every week acting as my girlfriend, and I would feed her any information I had on my progress. Her name was Agent Butkus. That part wasn't so bad—not bad at all.

The night before the transfer, my stomach was tangled in knots. My mind ran endlessly over every possible scenario, and I was weighed down with doubt. My mind raced back and forth with indecision about what I was getting myself into, and I didn't sleep a wink. The next morning, the guard came to collect me, and I could hear Geoff and Frank Jr. saying, "Good Luck on your appeal, man," and, "Give them hell. I don't want to see your face in here again."

The FBI agents and U.S. marshals shackled me up and loaded me in a van. Once we left the prison property, they removed my handcuffs, gave me a bag of clothes, and told me to change. They spoke to me as if I were just a normal person—none of that official police bullshit. We stopped at a family diner and had lunch. That small taste of freedom made me miss mine so much more. Once we were finished, we headed to the airport. We drove up to a private hangar where a small Learjet waited. *Hell,* I thought, eyeing the jet, *this will definitely be better than flying around in that Con Air plane. Certainly, more like what I'm used to.* When we got to Missouri, there were two more FBI agents waiting for us. They had me change my clothes again, but they didn't put the cuffs on me, and we all got into another van and headed out. We chatted about movies and music—normal everyday things that felt surreal compared to what I had waiting ahead of me.

Near the end of the drive, I glanced up and saw the prison looming in front of us. It looked like it belonged in a horror movie like some mid-evil castle. For the last time, my mind spun out of control, and I honestly wanted to back out. I briefly thought that maybe I could return to Milan and put my hope on my appeals like all the other prisoners did. But I wasn't a quitter, and I had a mission to accomplish: get in, get that sick fucker to confess, and get my life back. As the new prison guards were processing me in, I looked back at the U.S.

marshal who I had just been in the van with, and he gave me a furtive thumbs up for encouragement. With that, I embarked on my impossible mission.

Of course, I didn't manage to wait six months to talk to Larry Hall. Springfield can house more than a thousand prisoners at any given time, but I spotted him the very first time I went to the mess hall, and I even maneuvered myself close enough to bump into him and have a conversation. I knew I was walking on thin ice, but now that I had Hall right in front of me, my instincts took over, and luckily Beaumont had been right—I had just the right instincts to accomplish this crazy task. My gut told me that if I waited six whole months to talk to Hall, I might be too late. I felt that I should take any opportunity I was given to make progress, no matter when it presented itself.

I ended up in a cell right across from Hall, and before long, I was sitting with him and the other "baby killers" (men who had been convicted of child rape and murder) at every meal. Hall gave me the creeps in a serious way, and he wasn't easy to get talking about anything important, but he was already starting to seem comfortable with having me around.

The MCFP had a whole group of Mafia guys who were assigned there for violent murder charges rather than for being psychologically unstable. They were mostly big muscular men except for their leader Vincent "the Chin" Gigante, who was an elderly man of about seventy with a prominent jaw. Gigante was a former leader of the Genovese crime family in New York. He was an intelligent man who had managed to avoid incarceration for years by pretending to be mentally unstable. Being in a maximum-security prison didn't slow down Gigante's ability to manage Mafia affairs one bit. He was just as savvy as ever, and he had devised methods for passing information to his crew on the outside through veiled messages and signals.

Gigante saw me eating breakfast with Larry Hall and the other baby killers every morning, and maybe he identified me as someone who would fit into his little crime club because it wasn't long before he sent his men to collect me. As I finished my chow, and headed for the door, four of Gigante's cronies grabbed me and shuffled me down a corridor, I was ready to take them all on thinking it was a hit, but I soon seen that they had no shanks, or makeshift weapons. This was Gigante's way of saying hello. During our first conversation, he told me I needed to eat breakfast with his crew from that day on. That threw a big wrench in my plans to connect with Hall, but even among the disturbed and unpredictable prison population, Hall and the other men he hung around with were the lowest of the low. The other men at MCFP could see I wasn't really part of that group, and failing to follow the prison's social constructs could have jeopardized my mission or blown my cover. Gigante let me know in pretty direct words that hanging around with Hall and his sort would be a dangerous game, and once Gigante decided to have a hand in my prison life, I really couldn't tell him no.

I had deep connections and associates in the Chicago mob, but I was completely unknown to the mob in New York. I didn't know anything about Gigante at the time, but I soon learned about his dealings with the Mafia and decided that associating with him and his men could be a benefit and a protection if I played it right and stuck to my cover story. Even though he was still a powerful man, Gigante felt that prison life had crippled his mighty empire. He seemed to see himself much like a mistreated lion in a cage.

Gigante and his crew were pleasant enough to me, but I knew that associating with them was a dangerous game. Should they learn anything about my mission or realize that I wasn't everything I appeared to be, they wouldn't have hesitated to dispatch with me however it suited them. A shank in the back or a wire necktie were both likely possibilities.

Toiling away day after day in MCFP was maddening. My freedom felt so close, but securing it was like trying to grasp tiny minnows with my hands in a rushing river—it was near enough to touch, but reaching out to grab it would have been futile. Cracking into the skull of a full-blown madman like Larry Hall was not going to be easy. Hall was right under my nose, but the patience required to make any progress was difficult to maintain. As days passed, the soul-crushing monotony of prison life, with little variety and no way to escape the routines forced upon me wore at my psyche. But I always held firm in my resolve to complete my mission and secure my freedom.

I knew how to fix my sights on a goal and do everything required to accomplish it. My determination to make my fortune in the drug business had landed me where I was now, and that obviously wasn't the outcome I'd hoped for, but now I found that the skills I'd learned climbing that mountain to success were worth more to me now than all the money I'd lost.

I drew on my past experiences and knowledge like a vast reserve of water in a desert. It was almost like I was running through that barren wasteland in Arizona all over again with bullets whizzing around me, but this time it wasn't a day-long sprint, it was a months-long marathon. Running was easy—sitting and waiting proved to be a far greater challenge. Planning and strategizing my approaches to Hall, maintaining my cover, and building useful relationships with the dangerous men around me, were abilities people weren't just born with. But I'd been studying those skills for two decades, and I was a master.

This experience offered a whole new challenge, but I knew I was up for it, and I wasn't about to crumble under any circumstances. I would do what I'd always done—follow my instincts, look one step ahead, and get results.

I met a new roadblock when my bespectacled hacker friend Malcolm Shady from MCC turned up at MCFP unexpectedly to receive treatment for his kidney disease. He spotted me during mealtime with some of Gigante's crew and greeted me exuberantly. He was surprised to see me, and I knew right away that keeping my cover intact with Shady around would be a delicate dance. It was ironic, really—this identity thief could accidentally thwart my false, assumed persona without even realizing he was doing it.

"Hey, Shady! I said, smiling broadly at him. "What's new with you?"

"Oh, nothing much, Keene. What else new could there be? I'm still in jail. My kidney's acting up. I got sent to this place to get it cleared up. Glad it's just my kidney, though, and not my head. Some of these guys in here really give me the heebie-jeebies."

I forced an authentic-sounding laugh, wondering all the while how I would redirect the conversation next. I knew where this was going, and it wasn't going to be good.

"What about you?" Shady suddenly continued before I could stop him. "How's your drug conspiracy case shaking out? They send you here just for that? Or are you sick, too?" I grasped him firmly by the elbow and ushered him away from the table attempting to appear as casual as possible. I didn't look back. Showing that I was concerned about the mob men overhearing my conversation would only draw their interest.

"What're you thinking?" I whispered urgently through gritted teeth. "You think I want to talk about that here? Let it go, will you?"

"What's the big deal, Keene? I'm just wondering." Shady seemed taken aback, and then he left. My pulse pounded. Shady's presence here could become a serious, deadly problem. Hall was a twisted guy, but I wasn't his type—the other men around me were the real danger. If anyone smelled anything fishy about who I appeared to be, they would think I was a rat for sure.

I would never be an informant—I was sure about that. I'd been on the other side of that shit, and it made me crazy to think about it. I did want my freedom, but what I was doing now was about keeping a madman where he belonged—not about turning on the guys around me who had never done me any harm—but I didn't have any delusions about how easily they could do me in if they wanted to.

The photos of those girls Hall killed clung in my mind like a foul, lingering odor I couldn't shake. Those images were the spark that lit my fire and kept me going on this crazy endeavor. But the truth of my situation didn't matter an ounce as much as how I was perceived by my fellow prisoners. If they spotted anything about me that didn't add up, I couldn't just say, "Hey, guys. You can trust me. Sure, I'm running a gallant errand for the Feds, but you don't have anything to worry about. I won't utter a word to them about *you*." I could imagine how any one of those guys would respond. Each response would be different, but everyone would end with me having to take someone out, winding up maimed, or bleeding out somewhere with sirens blaring overhead.

I returned to the table to smooth over my awkward interaction with Shady and save face with Gigante and his men, and I didn't detect anything but bemused puzzlement from them about this friend of mine from a past facility. When I left our table, I took a deep breath feeling that I'd averted a crisis. For now.

But the next day, there was Shady again, "Hey, Keene! So, when are you going to give me the scoop? You told me all about your case back at MCC, and I wanna know how it turned out."

"Shady, I'm really not interested in talking about it, okay? Why do you care so much?"

"What else have we got to talk about around here?"

I shook him off again and changed the subject, but I knew that it was possible Shady would get comfortable with some of the other prisoners and start running his mouth in a bad way. If the New York Mafia guys got suspicious, I knew they would pressure Shady until he spilled everything he knew about me. Knowing the urgent danger of my situation and waiting for the right time to approach Hall filled my veins with a buzzing anxiety. I knew I had to make progress. If I didn't keep going, bit by bit, at every possible opportunity, I might explode or have this chance ripped from my grasp.

One time, I got impatient and decided to see if I could learn more about Hall by doing a little reconnaissance. I knew Hall's psychiatrist wouldn't share anything he'd told her, but I thought that maybe I could skip a few steps by reading her private notes and learning what he'd shared in their sessions. Maybe he'd even confessed to some things I could use. I went to Hall's psychiatrist's office and casually knocked on her door.

"Yes? Come in," she answered.

I popped my head in and said, "Oh, sorry. Wrong office." As my hand wrapped around the door, I stuffed a little wad of clay into the mechanism of the lock. It would prevent the lock from fully engaging and allow me to get in when no one was around.

A couple of nights later, I made my way back when the area was quiet back into the administrative restricted area. I carefully checked that the hallway was still and empty before I reached for the door handle and turned it. The door opened with a slight squeak of the hinges. I slipped inside silently and glanced around to locate a grey metal file cabinet in the corner. I opened the top drawer—nothing—and then the second drawer. Finally, my eyes fell upon the name I'd been searching for: Larry DeWayne Hall.

I slipped the file out and spread it open on the top of the cabinet. I flipped aside a few sheets, scanning medical forms and other notes for any pertinent information. I didn't find anything helpful at first, just a birthdate, allergies, mental treatment, and family medical history. I didn't find any notes that contained confessions of any kind. I gritted my teeth in frustration, knowing I was likely out of luck as I turned to the final stack of papers in the file. I froze.

It was a group of pencil drawings Hall had made. The pages were covered in the contorted, tied bodies of naked women. They twisted over the surfaces of the papers in silent agony. Their mouths and genitals were bloated and exaggerated like inflatable dolls. My mouth went dry. It was a disturbing reminder that the pudgy man I'd been trying to befriend really wasn't what he seemed. Larry Hall had dark secrets. He was dangerous and sick in ways I hadn't yet unearthed or ever encountered.

Suddenly, I heard boisterous laughter of prisoners echo in a nearby hallway. I tried to shake the images from the drawings out of my mind, but they left a haunting shadow behind as I quickly returned the file to its place looking as neat as I'd found it. I wiped down the few surfaces I'd touched with a clean sock and carefully snuck out of the room after removing the clay from the lock.

I was disappointed that my visit to the psychiatrist's office hadn't given me more information, but it did give me additional resolve. I continued to chip away at Hall's reserve and silence until he slowly opened up to me. Shady was continuing to question me about my drug conspiracy charges and appeals. It was only a matter of time before someone got suspicious. I knew my time was limited, and I had to get results—soon.

One night, I finally got Hall to talk. He told me about a girl named Laurie Depies whom he had met at a mall in Wisconsin. When he'd first approached her, she'd been friendly. Hall had believed she liked him, so he followed her out of the mall and then followed her car in his van. Laurie was driving to her boyfriend's apartment, and when she saw Hall approach her after she'd parked, she had become alarmed.

"She was very mean to me—not nice like she had been to me at the mall," Hall told me. His face clouded over with a dark empty expression then. He didn't say so, but he must have had chloroform ready when he left his van. He had a plan, and he knew what he wanted to do. He abducted Depies and drove away in his van to a quiet area nearby. He said he didn't remember anything after that. He blacked out and found himself in a dream state hovering above her, but he said he was doing bad things. When he came to, he was lying next to her naked form on the floor of his van. He buried her lifeless body in southern Wisconsin.

I learned later that her boyfriend had heard Depies' noisy car drive up outside the apartment complex, but when she never arrived and he found her car left behind with no trace of Depies, he called the police. The only evidence left behind was Depies' drink still full of ice sitting on the roof of her Volkswagen Rabbit.

Hall told me more and more as the days wore on, and he came to trust me almost as if I were a surrogate brother or his personal protector. He admitted to me that he had murdered Tricia Reitler and Jessica Roach, and he shared specific details about how he'd killed them. He mentioned other women and girls as well over the course of several months.

One particularly horrific incident he related became embedded in my memory. He said he'd murdered a young mother in Indianapolis named Michelle Dewey.

She had been sunbathing in her yard as her young son played nearby. Hall had seen her and pulled up to the curb. He said he was trying to find an address to buy some motor parts and asked to use her phone. She agreed, but once inside, he tried to abduct her. Again, he told me she had been "mean" to him, and he'd had to strangle her. He had another out-of-body experience until her toddler's alarmed cries snapped him out of it. Rather than take Dewey's body, he put the child in a closet and fled the scene, leaving Michelle and the unharmed boy behind for an unwitting babysitter to find.

Listening to Hall talk about what he'd done was a painful, sickening experience. I knew I was close—so close—to completing my mission. Now I just had to get him to tell me where he had left his victims' bodies. This was harder information to obtain without making Hall nervous, especially since he'd told me how careful he'd been while burying the evidence. It was almost like he felt possessive over the women—as if they'd been his treasures that he didn't want anyone else to steal away. He said he would one day reunite with them in another life. He didn't want anyone knowing or discovering where they were, and he was clearly used to keeping that information strictly to himself.

Due to knowledge gained in his janitorial jobs and from working in a cemetery his whole life, he'd buried most of the bodies with a special cocktail of dissolving acidic chemicals that would cause quick decomposition and turn the bodies to ash. If they ever were found, he made it sound like there wouldn't be much of anything left. Hall had even shared with me how he'd made homemade chloroform from starter fluid, ether, and other chemicals to help subdue his victims. He was beginning to trust me more and more, but in the meantime, I had begun to sense suspicion from Gigante and his men.

At lunch one day, they seemed more terse than usual and less relaxed in their conversation with each other. One of Gigante's guys—a guy named Vinny—turned to me with a stale slice of bread gripped in his meaty fist. "So, Keene. How's that weapons case against you going?" He paused. "Or wait—it was weapons, right?" His eyes glinted.

The hairs on the back of my neck bristled, but I was an old hand at keeping my cool. "It's bad, man. My attorneys are working on it, but there's not much hope." I shot him a disarming smile. "Why? You got a way to help me out?"

Vinny's lips stretched into a broad grin. "Maybe, Keene. Maybe I *can* help you *out*." The last word carried unsettling weight. Then he smiled again and slapped me on the back. I knew right then that my time was up.

After I left the mess hall, I decided I had to do something. Normally, I wasn't allowed in the wood shop, but Hall spent most of his extra time there, so I snuck in.

Spending time in that shop was one of the many privileges Hall enjoyed just because he had useful skills and could fix things around the facility.

It was strange how a man as twisted and sick as Larry Hall could be such a model prisoner. It seemed he was capable of following every rule the world threw at his warped mind until it came to not violently destroying the lives of innocent young women. Sure, he was a creep, but why was that the thing he didn't seem to be able to manage? What the hell caused a man like Hall to be like he was? I didn't know, but I intended to do everything in my power to keep him from ever killing again. My life depended on it now.

I snuck toward the bench where Hall was working intently on a project. Hall clutched a small figure in his hand. He patiently carved away at the details with deliberate, reverent precision. As it often was, his mind seemed absorbed in a private, meditative state. Thinking about what was going on in that mind of his made my skin crawl. I swallowed my disgust and moved closer until I could see that the wooden figure cradled in Hall's hand was a bird of some kind with a long, hooked beak.

I took in more of the scene on Hall's bench and realized he had a whole group of birds all lined up on top of a paper speckled with red dots.

"Hi, Larry."

Hall jumped and turned to block my view of the workbench. "Oh, hi, James. What are you doing here? You shouldn't be here."

I put on a casual, mischievous demeanor and explained how the guard at the door had been absent and how I'd decided to drop in and pay him a visit. I reached out nonchalantly and picked up one of the small carvings. Larry's eyes flashed suddenly, and he balled his right fist and slammed it firmly on the table.

"Hey, I'm just looking. I'll give it right back," I said reassuringly. A moment of silence later, his sudden storm had passed, and he'd returned to his regular sedate expression.

"Wow, you're pretty good at this stuff, right? What are they, Larry? Did you make them all yourself?"

Hall nodded. He looked anxious to retrieve the bird from my hand, but instead, he stroked its head as it lay in my palm. "They're falcons. I'm sending them to my brother."

"Why? What're they for?"

What Hall said next is already common knowledge to most people who know my story, but it was the key to everything: "They watch over the dead." My blood turned to ice. Then an electric jolt ran through my body from head to toe. This was it. That paper was a homemade map, and Hall must have marked where each body was hidden. He was sending these falcons home to his brother to put at the burial sites as some sort of sick personal tribute to his murdered victims. The map was lying there right in front of me. It took all of the self-control I had not to snatch it right out of his grasp. Instead, I maintained a casual appearance and pretended to watch Hall work as I considered my options.

Gigante was onto me—I was sure of it. I knew I had to contact the FBI right away. I made my excuses to Larry and ran to call Agent Butkus on her direct line. I was certain she'd get back to me immediately. Our fabricated relationship was plenty convincing by that time, and I knew she was on my side and wanted what was best for me.

The phone rang and rang, but she didn't answer. I had to leave a voicemail. I explained what I'd discovered, but now I was in a panic. If she didn't get the information soon enough, I would still be vulnerable to the Mafia in the meantime. I figured she'd hear it in time to intercept the map and the wooden falcons before they made it to Hall's brother, but I had to do something drastic before then, or I would be a sitting duck. Adrenaline pumped through my veins, and as I calculated my options, I made a plan—a crazy plan. *Oh, this is really going to suck*, I thought. *But at least I'll be able to get a few things off my chest*. I had to do it. The game was over, my freedom was so close I could taste it, but it wouldn't do me any good if Gigante's men took me out before I could hightail it out of that shithole.

I found Hall in his cell. I strode right in, direct and confident—unlike any way I'd ever approached Hall before. I could see in his eyes that he understood something had changed between us. Right then, I unloaded everything I thought about him. I didn't spare any details. I told him what a sick, monstrous, psychopath he was to kill young girls as they cried for their mothers.

He lost it. He slid his chair back away from me and trembled, stuttering, "Beaumont sent you. Didn't he. Beaumont sent you." His eyes welled up with tears. The bell for lockdown sounded, and I returned to my cell for the night fully expecting my plan to play out and preserve my safety if the Feds didn't arrive in time.

As I suspected, Larry Hall used his influence with the guards to get out of his cell and contact his shrink, who coddled and babied him. She came to my cell the next morning with a fleet of guards to assist her. They barged in before dawn. As she marched through the parted group of uniformed men, I still lay in my bunk wrapped in my itchy gray blanket. She pointed her finger in my face.

"Who are you?"

I blinked blearily. "I'm inmate James Keene, 110026."

"No. That's not what I mean," she snapped. "Who sent you here? Who do you work for?"

"I have no idea what you're talking about."

She scoffed and turned to the guards. "Take him to solitary confinement until I get to the bottom of this." They dragged me off before breakfast. I hadn't been released, but I was hopeful I would be soon. At least for now I was alone. That meant I was safe.

Solitary was a horribly bad place to be, but I'd come this far—I could do one more night. I was sure the FBI would bust me out in the morning. But morning came and went.

The next day, Hall's psychiatrist showed up to continue interrogating me. She accused me of being sent by Beaumont to get information, but I didn't tell her anything, and she didn't let me out. That day turned into another, and those days turned into weeks. They were some of the darkest, coldest weeks of my life, and I had no idea what was going on. After all I'd survived, I wondered if I'd lost everything I had going for me once again. Hadn't Agent Butkus received the message? Was the FBI planning to leave me down here to rot? Where was Hall's map? Was I to be forever lost in the system as my dad feared?

Hour after hour stretched into what felt like an eternity. I had to negotiate for everything I needed from the guards in there, and I finally succeeded in getting them to bring my psychiatrist down. He was my only contact within the prison, and I soon learned he'd been on vacation the whole time. I was furious, but he finally got me out. Unfortunately, I learned that Agent Butkus didn't get the message and that Hall's map was gone. All of my evidence had gone up in smoke, but the Feds understood the danger I was in, and they still pulled me out of Springfield.

Even though the map was gone, Agent Butkus advocated tirelessly for my release. She said I'd done all that I could, that I had succeeded in gleaning valuable confessions from Hall that included details only the actual killer could have known, and that I had fulfilled my part in the deal.

Beaumont asked if I would submit to a polygraph to verify the valuable corroborating evidence I had obtained. I'd also told them about the map and about everything else Hall had said in great detail. I gladly agreed to the polygraph. Beaumont was renowned for his ability to administer and read a lie detector test, and I passed with flying colors. The Feds were happy to have further details and confessions from Hall, but they didn't know what to make of my story about the map and the wooden birds, so they more or less dismissed it. The FBI felt bad about the time I'd spent in solitary, so while we waited for my sentencing judge to review my case, they agreed to send me back to Milan.

I wasn't free yet, but I was so close, it felt like I was knocking on heaven's door. When I arrived at Milan, Geoff and Frank Sr. were happy to see me. I'd told them the Feds had transferred me there temporarily while I was waiting for my appeal to be approved and that I would probably be leaving. Geoff told me he'd won his appeal and would also be released soon. I was ecstatic for Geoff. That kid had gone through hell.

Both Frank and I were happy for him, but Frank's reaction was much more subdued. As we spoke about the possibility that Geoff and I would both soon be free men, resigned tears began to stream down Frank's face. I couldn't read his thoughts, but the hopeless expression etched on his face was easy to decipher. Frank knew he didn't have a chance of leaving that place. He would stay in prison for the rest of his life. I knew that the new flame of hope I held inside was truly priceless.

CHAPTER 13

THE TOP OF THE MOUNTAIN

My official release finally arrived on a sweltering day in August. My clothes had been packed up and sent to my dad after I was sentenced, so the guards gave me a pair of jeans and a T-shirt to go home in. It wasn't much—certainly not the sort of clothing I would have picked for myself, but I didn't care. It was the last thing on my mind.

When I walked out of that prison for the final time into the hot summer air, it felt like a mountain of crushing weight was lifted off my shoulders. I knew about weight, and I knew about strength. I'd lifted a lot of weights in prison, and that kind of resistance will build you into a stronger, more resilient person—but the weight of incarceration wasn't like that—that had been the kind of weight that was impossible to escape no matter how tough you were. That was the sort of weight that crushed your soul while your body—as physically strong as ever—stood by helpless.

After all of the hard things that happened in my family when I was a kid, and after twenty years of dodging peril while running a thriving drug empire, I thought I'd seen it all. But I'd still seen and heard things in prison that were impossible to forget—things that showed me how monstrous and evil a human being could become, even if he seemed harmless enough on the outside. The thought that I could have spent ten whole years in that death and despair-choked place filled me with a deep revulsion.

I had started my journey in life desperate to climb to the top of the mountain of success and financial freedom even though the path I'd chosen was off the beaten path and a dangerous one. I thought that money was the answer to all of my family's problems, and I set out to change our fortunes at almost any cost and as quickly as I knew how.

All of the rich people I saw seemed to have it easy. Their lives looked perfect—full of glamour, ease, fancy cars, and gorgeous people. People like them had respect and influence. I felt that acquiring everything they had would give me and my family sweet freedom. I was a smart, enterprising kid, and the pervasive crime in my hometown and the surrounding area presented me with what I thought was the ideal solution. When I spotted those bags in that cornfield all those years ago, I had grabbed that chance and held onto it with everything I had. But that lifestyle had backfired in a big way and landed me lower than I ever thought possible. I fought through the trial and the family tragedy we went through, but the thriving business I had built erupted in flames around me. It looked like I was doomed to be a casualty of the fallout.

Then, in what was a most unlikely twist of fate, Beaumont—the man who had lit the match—came along with an impossible proposition, and once again, I hung onto that chance with vice-like determination and used every ounce of strength and cunning I'd gained over the years to see it through. I'd crawled through hell and fire on my belly, but now I had emerged from the ashes.

Now I was free.

And let me tell you, freedom tasted good. No amount of money in the world could replace it. Not only was I free from prison, but I was also free from my criminal record and free from everything that ended me up in that situation in the first place. The only thing I had left—the only thing that had ever mattered—was my family.

Dad, my brother, Tim, and my sister, Terri, made the three-hour drive to pick me up. As I walked toward them through the prison gates, we were all speechless—hardly able to believe that this day had finally come or that it had come in the strange way it had. I stopped a few feet from Dad, and a huge grin spread across my face.

He stared back at me, and he grinned as well. The way his lips still drooped on one side from the stroke he'd suffered didn't matter. His face still emanated pure joy.

"Jimmy!" he cried in his booming voice, and I closed the distance between him and wrapped him in my arms. We held each other in a firm embrace despite the sweltering heat, laughing with such abandon that I thought my heart would burst.

"Hey, Dad. Think you can handle having me around again so soon?" I joked. "I guess you'll have to make a little more time in your schedule for your firstborn now.

"I guess so, Jimmy! I'll adjust, son." I'd always loved it when my dad called me son. That word held a deep meaning for me that no other term of endearment could ever replace. When Dad was gone, I never stopped hearing it in my head and missing it. We pulled back and smiled at each other again. It was so good to see him standing there healthy and whole again. He'd been changed by this experience, just like I had been, and it showed. But he was still the man I loved and looked up to above all others, and the pride in his expression was the greatest possible gift I could have received that day—that day of sweet freedom!

I greeted my siblings next, crushing them with hugs and relishing the ability to be in their presence without a guard keeping watch or knowing they'd soon be gone. When we finished enjoying our reunion, Tim asked,

"Well, now what? You're a free man. What's the first thing you're going to do?"

I didn't have to think very long. "Food," I said "*Real* food, please. The best seafood place we can find—*now!*" Everyone laughed. After months and months of meager prison cuisine, my body craved quality food like a plant in darkness craves sunlight.

"That sounds just fine," Dad said. "Let's go."

We found a place with fresh seafood, and I ordered a fish fillet that had been grilled and squeezed with tart lemon and served with tender buttered vegetables and beautifully seasoned rice. It tasted like heaven—I couldn't remember a time when food had tasted so good. I ate so much that I could barely move. I nearly had to crawl to the car afterward.

As we ate, Terri teased me about my prison physique.

"Good thing the food was so bad. If they'd fed you any better in there, you'd be a monster! Look at all that muscle! Your arms are huge!"

"Nah," Dad said. "He looks great. He looks like the strong, talented athlete he's always been." His face practically glowed, and I knew he felt as free that day as I did.

Back in Chicago, I didn't have a house to go to. Dad took me home with him, but his wife didn't like me living with them, despite the fact that I'd actually been the one to buy the damn house. It was still in my name in the blind trust my dad and I had created. After enduring her complaining for a little while, I moved in with Terri. When Dad died a few years later, the 1.6-million-dollar house and properties were mortgaged to the hilt, and what was left of their value only came out to thirty thousand dollars. I didn't feel that Dad's wife had any right to even that small amount of money, especially since I'd already lost everything, but I let her have it anyway.

Living with Terri turned out to be a lot more fun. I was more than eager to get my game back on, and Terri had plenty of beautiful friends. One of her friends, named Monica, immediately caught my eye. Monica was a tall, leggy brunette with large, green eyes and a light dusting of freckles across her soft, creamy complexion. I still remember the first time I saw her. She strolled into Monica's place with her long, curvy legs wearing a sheer, silky blouse and a miniskirt, and all of a sudden, my hard-won freedom was even more delicious.

"Hey, you must be Jimmy," she said, and one corner of her mouth curved slyly upward. "Terri's told me you're quite the ladies' man. That true?" Her figure was something else, and she knew certainly knew how to catch a man's attention.

I shrugged and flashed her my winning smile. "Doesn't seem like something you should take Terri's word for," I said. "I'll let you make up your own mind." She took me up on the offer.

Monica was a kind person, but she also had that spark of mischief that meant she loved to have a good time. We hit it off, and before long I'd moved in with her. I stayed there for about eight months while I got back on my feet.

I didn't have anything left of my former businesses when I came out of Springfield, and that was okay. All of my money was gone. My real estate development company was still around, but only because I'd had a guy there keeping my license current. It wasn't doing very well or making any money. I decided to build it back up, but I knew I needed something else in the meantime.

I approached the guy who had purchased my car dealership. He knew I understood the car business and all of the necessary details, so he offered me a sales job on the spot. I made pretty decent money selling exotic cars, especially through commissions. I was still one hell of a businessman. But it was nothing like I'd been used to before.

Knowing how to restart after spending time in prison isn't an easy thing. The difficulty of it crushes many ex-prisoners, and they never fully adapt to living back in society. I still had a host of specialized skills any Mafia family or drug lord would have found highly useful. I'd made plenty of connections with Mafia guys in prison, and I knew they'd be interested in having me work for them. It would have been an easy path to follow, and there were times when my old life came around to visit, but I had no interest in inviting it to stay. Sometimes I saw former associates from my drug business, but I made it clear to all of them that I was out of the game—for good. For the most part, everyone respected that decision and left me alone.

The Mafia guys I'd been involved with before my arrest approached me with a proposition that would have been tempting to my past self. They wanted me to run their casinos, and after hour clubs, it was very tempting, and a glimmer of my past partying life, with naked waitress's and a constant party atmosphere. They respected me, especially since I had kept my mouth shut and never ratted on anyone. They saw me as a powerful guy whose influence they could use in their establishments, and they said they'd give me 1.5 million a year just to lend my endorsement.

As tempting as the money was, it was an offer I was happy to refuse. By this time, the mob in Chicago was dealing with their own law enforcement trouble, so they never pressured me about it. They made it clear that the offer remained on the table if I was ever interested, but I wasn't. That was a road I knew I would never go down again.

I knew my dangerous undercover mission had been a lifeline that helped me to escape some of the hardships ex-cons face coming back into regular life. I could have ended up much worse off than I did. Not only did I get years of my life back thanks to my decision to accept the deal, I got a chance to start over that wouldn't have come around twice.

Most people leave prison with a public record and few or no connections to help them out. Most businesses aren't eager to hire someone who has spent ten years behind bars. If I'd stayed in Milan for my full ten-year sentence, working for the mob would probably have been where I would have landed afterward. The skills I'd built over the years were exactly the sort of skills they could have used to their advantage. I was friendly with the mob guys in Milan, and if I had come out of prison as a convict, I wouldn't have had many other good options or places to go.

But I couldn't imagine going back to that sort of life again. I knew how good freedom tasted, and there was not a chance in hell I ever wanted to find myself in prison again—even for one day. I still had drive, and I still had the motivation to succeed, so I knew that whatever I did next would keep me solidly out of trouble. I didn't want anything to do with drugs or money-hungry people who lived life on the careless edge. I'd seen far too much of that shit. I wanted to live a life I could be proud of. I knew that all of my business dealings for the rest of my life would be honest, and that would be good enough.

I'm still grateful that I never got back into selling marijuana. That life was exciting, perilous, and addictive. It's part of my story, and I want to tell it. But the marijuana business now has changed and grown darker and more destructive. Back when I got involved in the business, it was completely different.

Today's drugs are bad news. They're harder, more powerful, and more habit-forming than the weed I sold back in the eighties and nineties. The overall potency varies, but the THC in marijuana in 2008 was measured to be as much as five times stronger than it used to be. I can imagine it's only getting more potent as time goes on.

In today's drug world, there are dangers like fentanyl, a potent and deadly ingredient that drug producers are cutting into everything. There's also an opioid crisis, and when people can't score painkillers, they turn to heroin—another devastating killer. Meth is made from ingredients so dangerous that it will rot the bones from inside of you and cause your teeth to disintegrate. Users are getting younger and younger, too. The average age that users start is ten to thirteen. By the time those kids are fully developed, there is a strong likelihood that they will be addicts for life. I wouldn't want anything to do with selling today's drugs.

After my release, no one knew what I'd been through except my friends and close family. Sometimes the memory of the wild ride I'd had took my breath away, and I wondered if I should tell my story. Dad said it should be a movie. Most people I shared that idea with thought I was crazy, but my dad believed that everyone would listen and be captivated by all that I'd experienced.

I'd had a brush with Hollywood years before in 1986 during the filming of *The Color of Money* starring Paul Newman and Tom Cruise. The production crew filmed some of the scenes in a pool hall in the same part of Chicago I was living in at the time. I decided to go down to the set to see about being cast.

Inside the pool hall, people were running around everywhere—building set pieces, adding finishing touches to every prop and furnishing, planning the lighting, and doing all kinds of things. I couldn't believe the number of people involved in the whole production. The atmosphere was electric, and I loved every bit of it. It was a career I had often wanted to be in since I was a young kid.

I asked around about being an extra, and someone told me to meet with the casting director the next morning. I called my brother Tim and asked him if he wanted to go to the casting call with me, so Tim and I showed up first thing the next day and met with the casting director in her office.

"Well, you look like what we need, that's for sure," she'd told us, eyeing us up and down appraisingly. She looked pleased. "Anything else about you we need to know?"

We told her we were skilled pool players, and she cast us as extras right away.

During filming, I met Martin Scorsese, who was the director. He must have seen how much I loved being there, and he seemed to think I had presence and charisma. He chatted with me for a while a few times, and at one point he told me, "Jimmy, you know what? You have everything Tom Cruise has. You just need the right opportunity to be discovered." But that was where our conversation ended. As he walked off, Tim came up behind me and grabbed my shoulder.

"You hear that, Jimmy? Did you hear what he said about you and Tom Cruise? Scorsese loves you!" I enjoyed the compliment, but I wished I'd said something—anything—to take the conversation further. I couldn't believe I hadn't seized that chance while I'd had it in my hands. I wanted to command Scorsese's attention and say, "Be that opportunity I need—you can make something happen for me." But I didn't, and that was where it ended—at least for the time being.

Later, after my release from prison, I decided to reach out to a publishing agent in New York City, and I sent him a one-page summary of my experiences in Springfield. He was immediately intrigued.

"Mr. Keene, this is an unbelievable story. You actually did this? You lived through this?" He was dumbfounded.

"Yeah," I responded. "And that barely scratches the surface, honestly."

"Do you mind if I send this to a few people in Hollywood? This would make one hell of a movie." I agreed, and that's what he did. Within twenty-four hours, several major studios were clamoring for the movie rights, and a little while later, I had a movie deal. Dad would have been ecstatic. We had lost him right before this deal came through. I always looked at it as a sign from heaven saying, "*Let me give you a hand son.*"

In an interesting twist of fate, Martin Scorcese signed on to direct it. I told some of the executives I spoke with at Paramount that I'd done *The Color of Money*, and they said Scorcese remembered me. I don't know whether or not that was true, but it was interesting to hear. They cast Brad Pitt to play me originally, which was really great. But there were issues with the script and other delays, and I eventually decided to start by publishing a book.

Putting my experiences down on paper felt like a new kind of freedom. My life so far had been full of insane twists and turns, and I loved seeing part of my story turned into a polished, published story that would finally be available for people to read. When I released my first book in September 2010, it became popular immediately, and suddenly everyone was talking about events my family and I had been carrying around on our own for years.

Reporters started calling to write articles and cover the details of what I'd experienced. It wasn't long before CNN, *Dateline,* Paula Zahn, and several others approached me about making specials based on my story. *Playboy* even wrote a piece about me that became their featured article of the year.

My time in Springfield had not been much of a picnic—quite the contrary—but I was glad to get as much truth about Larry Hall out there as I could, especially if any of it would help keep him safely behind bars and away from innocent little girls for the rest of his life. I knew it wasn't much, but I hoped that knowing more about Hall's admissions of guilt would offer his victims' families at least some small amount of closure.

After I left Springfield and before the release of my book, I got a call from a couple of cold case detectives that were working on the Michelle Dewey case in Indiana and several other unsolved murders involving Larry Hall. They asked me to come to Indianapolis to talk to them about Larry Hall in detail.

When I arrived, each and every seasoned and hard-nosed detective hugged me and thanked me on behalf of all law enforcement for the heroic, outstanding job I had done in securing Larry Hall's fate so he could never kill again. All the law enforcement I have encountered—FBI, local police and detectives, U.S. attorneys, and chief state judges—have been wonderfully appreciative and congratulatory for all I did in stopping the monster Larry Hall.

The cold case detectives in Indiana first showed me hand-drawn pictures by Larry Hall of women and girls being sexually tortured and exploited in sick and twisted variations, just like the bizarre drawings I had found in the psychiatrist's office cabinets at Springfield. This had obviously been a long-term obsession for Hall. I wondered whether the sketches were merely a morbid fantasy or whether they depicted actual victims or plans Hall had been making. The detectives then showed me a long video they had made of their visit and raid upon Hall's home after his initial arrest. The detectives asked me to study the inside of Hall's home and tell them anything I noticed.

Seeing the inside of Hall's home from years before was haunting and surreal. The video showed a torn-up truck motor strewn over the floor of a room. Black grease streaked the carpet, and the tangle of auto parts looked chaotic but also methodical—like the obsessive person who'd put them there had painstakingly arranged each one according to his own, mad set of rules.

There was also footage of a walk-in closet containing more auto parts, some clothing on hangers, and a five-foot-tall dresser with two shelves above it. The shelves contained a number of "memorabilia" items Hall had presumably collected from his victims—including a photo album that had belonged to Michelle Dewey. As I watched the camera pan over the contents of the closet, my eyes suddenly caught on a cluster of small, detailed wooden birds nestled in the corner of a box—the falcons.

"I know what those are," I told the detectives.

They wanted to hear everything.

A few years later, the detectives contacted me again and told me they wanted to go after Hall for Dewey's murder and get him the death penalty. Larry Hall killed far more women and girls than he ever told me about. Researchers and detectives later surmised that Hall had killed around fifty-four women and girls between the ages of ten and fifty-nine. He had traveled around like a predator for ten years ending the lives of women from all walks of life including little girls on their bikes, young mothers, and prostitutes.

Of the fifty-four, Hall only admitted to fifteen, and fourteen total bodies were found that were likely Hall's victims. The rest of the women seemed to have disappeared into thin air without a trace, leaving all of their personal belongings behind. I continue to hope that more and more victims will have their stories uncovered—one way or another.

If I learned anything by the time I left prison, it was that the things I thought had mattered really weren't so important. Dad died on November 28, 2004, but I was able to spend five more wonderful years with him. Tim and I took him on fishing trips to Canada to escape the city—as much as we loved it—and soak in the simple eloquence of nature. There was nothing like standing on the shore of a glassy mountain lake together, laughing, enjoying the sunshine, and casting our lines out over the still water.

One perfect evening, as we watched the sunrise over snowcapped Canadian mountains and listened to the landscape teeming with life around us, Dad said, "You know, we've been through a lot together, son. Thanks for always helping me out like you have. I know I wasn't the easiest business partner to have over the years. I know you had to bail me out more than once. You don't know much that all meant to me, and I'm sorry I put you through all that I did. From the bottom of my heart, I'm sorry, son."

"Dad, you don't need to mention it ever again. It doesn't matter anymore. It's all done and over with. I made mistakes, too. You know that."

We gazed silently ahead as a flock of geese flew over the luminous lake and came in low until they skimmed across the water's surface and settled there to float and dive for their dinner.

Then, I spoke. "Let's make a pact here and now. We'll never talk about money again."

Dad's eyes twinkled, and he turned to look at me with a soft smile. "Okay, son. Deal." And that was that.

Dad and I didn't waste any more time in our relationship talking about finances or business ventures. We never spoke about those things again. Instead, we just enjoyed each other and honed our fly-fishing skills.

"Your whole story will get out there one day," Dad told me once on another fishing trip to Minnesota. "Remember what Martin Scorsese said? He was right! You could have been as big as Tom Cruise."

"I know, Dad. I remember." I shook my head and chuckled. "You've always had my back."

Dad was my biggest supporter, just like he had been all of my life, despite the times I'd disappointed him. He still believed I could do anything and be anyone. He believed I could move mountains and that someday I would reach that mountaintop. I've walked with powerful men, legends, and giants, but no one could ever cast a shadow over my father—or ever will.

The last few years I spent with him were worth everything I risked when I agreed to make Larry Hall and Springfield a part of my story. He never saw my published book or anything else that came out of that hellish experience, but I can imagine how proud he would have been to see me on the news, hear my interviews, or to read my books. He would have told everyone he knew about it, and he would have laughed in that big, booming voice of his. Sometimes, I can still hear it.

My life became much calmer but also adventurous in a different way. My real estate development company grew and thrived under my focused care. I loved telling my exhilarating life story as I created new books and films. They allowed me to live vicariously through the screen without dodging bullets or having to talk myself or members of my crew out of a deadly tight spot. I didn't need to actually be an FBI agent or a spy or my old self—I could watch someone be that on a screen where everyone could enjoy it without getting hurt or risking my neck. I still loved that environment that I found so tantalizing when I was cast in *Color of Money*.

My story was adapted as the miniseries *Black Bird* by Apple TV+ in July 2022 and finally made it to the screen. The show was developed by the outstanding Dennis Lehane and had a first-rate cast, including Taron Egerton, Paul Walter Hauser, Sepideh Moafi, Greg Kinnear, and Ray Liotta. It made the top-ten list of most-streamed shows in the United States for weeks in a row and was an instant hit.

Seeing the project completed felt euphoric, and it received excellent reviews. *Black Bird* was nominated for three Golden Globe awards, including Best Television Limited Series, and Paul Walter Hauser won a Golden Globe and a Critic's Choice Television award for Best Supporting Actor for his performance as Larry Hall. Both Taron Egerton and Paul Walter Hauser were nominated for Screen Actors Guild awards.

I'd spent ten years trying to get that project out to the public, and when I finally did, it was wonderful to see the finished result and hear how much people enjoyed it. I attended the 2022 world premiere release of the series in person to celebrate the show's success, and I even made a cameo appearance in the final episode.

I knew that scene would have been Dad's favorite.

One late afternoon, years after I met Larry Hall, my phone rang.

"Is this James Keene?"

"Yeah. What can I do for you?"

"This is Chief Judge John Ericsman. I'm working with the FBI on a bizarre case involving a highly dangerous serial killer. We have issues we just can't resolve, and we're hoping you'll give us some insight and help us with this case."

I hadn't seen that one coming. Maybe my dream from long ago about getting into law enforcement wasn't going to let me go so easily after all. "I've had my fill of serial killers," I said.

"I'm sure that's true, Mr. Keene, but that's exactly why we need your help. Please. This guy has us baffled. We're stuck in a serious rut here. This psychopath is a long-distance truck driver. He's been collecting victims all across the country like postage stamps and leaving their dead bodies behind."

Without warning, I felt the grim, uneasy feeling that became so familiar to me when I was hanging around with Larry Hall return to my gut as if it had never left. "He sounds like a real winner."

"Yeah, that's right—a real upstanding citizen. We'd like you to come meet with us and act as a consultant."

I considered for a moment, remembering a certain file of grisly, haunting photographs. I thought about someone new building a similar album of morbid crime-scene images, and the uneasy feeling in my gut was replaced with another familiar feeling—firm resolve. As long as they weren't asking me to investigate from *behind* prison bars again, I decided I might as well see how I could help. "Sure. I'm in."

And just like that, I was headed off on another wild ride.

PHOTO
ILLUSTRATIONS

Mom & Dad's wedding. Mom is 8 months pregnant with me.
Such a great looking couple!

My Beautiful Mom   Big Jim Keene

"Jimmy" Eastside Bulldogs
junior league

Eastside Junior Ball
"Jimmy the Speedster"

Big Jim receiving an honorary
award for Bravery
in the Line of Duty

My Dad the Hero!

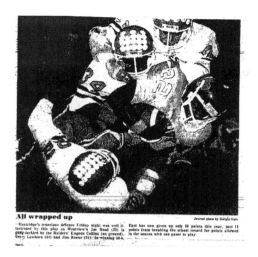

All wrapped up

Journal photo by Dwight Nale

—Eastridge's tenacious defense Friday night was well illustrated by this play as Westview's Joe Hood (32) is gang-tackled by the Raiders' Eugene Collins (on ground), Terry Lawhorn (34) and Jim Koenz (51); in winning 28-6. East has now given up only 28 points this year, just 12 points from breaking the school record for points allowed in the season with one game to play.

The caption says it all. My Eastridge team breaking records

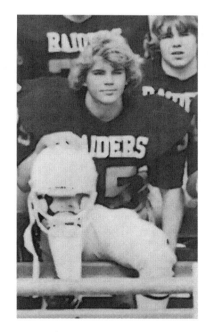

Freshmen Year at Eastridge

MVP

Can't drive 55 in my 6,6 Trans Am 16 years old

Working out with 8-time Mr. Olympia Lee Haney

Wild Times at my Brownstone

My Passion for Corvettes

Reminiscing about the old Football days at the home field.

Lifelong Dedication to Martial Arts

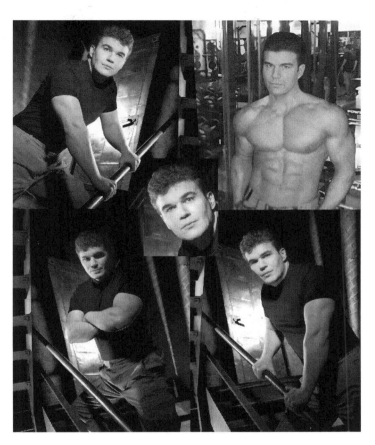

On Top of My Game

Jimmy & Taron on *Black Bird* set having a few laughs

On set with *Black Bird* Golden-Globe Winner Paul Walter Hauser

ACKNOWLEDGMENTS

I'd like to give special thanks to my Superman father, "Big Jim" Keene, and my mother, Lynn Keene. Thanks to Timothy "Timmy" Keene, Terri Lynn Keene, Sarina Keene, Valerie Keene, Margaret "Aunt Sis" Keene, Corey Keene, "Aunt Ginger" Brower, as well as to Kathy Psikos, Rick Carter, Kelly Brault, and Joan Obial.

I'm also grateful to Apple TV+ film studios, who really made things happen, as well as to my close friends and esteemed film professionals Bradley Thomas, Alexandra Milchan, Dennis Lehane, Kary Antholis, Richard Plepler, Scott Lambert, Michael Roskam, Joe Chappelle, Dan Friedkin, Ryan Friedkin, and Joel Gotler.

Thank you to Taron Egerton, Paul Walter Hauser, Sepideh Moafi, Greg Kinnear, and the late, great Ray Liotta for their outstanding performances in *Black Bird*.

Thank you to Anna Davis and her team at Glacier Media Marketing and Silly Goat Media for all their hard work and expertise.

Finally, thank you to the best friends a guy could ask for—Paul Desmarteau, Mark Capriotti, Scott Themer, Steve Themer, James "Jimmy" Olshefski, John "Johnny" Olshefski, Robert "Bobby" Ferrias, Lance Davis, Rick Carter, Kelly Brault, Michael Andrews, Bryan Andrews, Geoff Wiitala, Bob Anderson, and Phyllis Chudik.